MW01452222

Racing LANCIAS

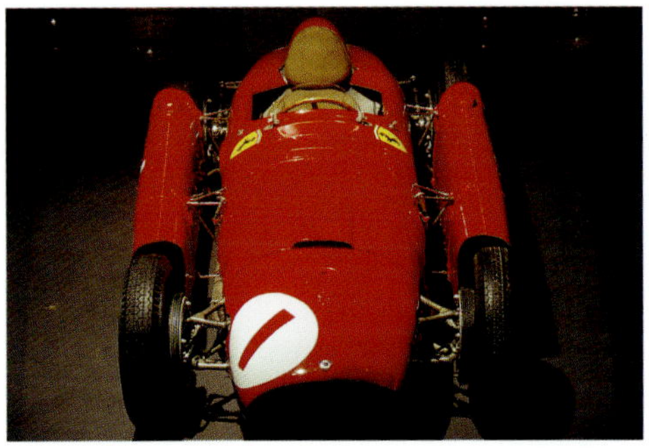

GIANCARLO REGGIANI

Racing
LANCIAS

GIORGIO NADA EDITORE

Giorgio Nada Editore s.r.l.

Editorial coordination
Luciano Greggio

Photographs and text
Giancarlo Reggiani

Cover
Giorgio Nada Editore

Translation
Robert Newman

The author and editor would like to thank the following people for their kind assistance:
Paolo Alessi, Miki Biasion, Lorenzo Bresolin, Angelo Del Monte, Ezio Facchinello, Claudio and Nicola Maglioli, Antonio Pasquale, Giorgio Schon, Silvano Toni, the Lancia Press Office and Historical Archives, the Ferrari Press Office, the Martini & Rossi Press Office, Giuseppe Volta.

© 2001 Giorgio Nada Editore, Vimodrone (MI)
printed in Italy

All rights reserved. Apart from any fair dealing for the purpose of private study, research, criticism or review, no part of this publication may be reproduced, stored in a retrieval system, or transmitted, by any means, electronic, electrical, chemical, mechanical, optical photocopying, recording or otherwise, without prior written permission. All enquiries should be addressed to the publisher:

Giorgio Nada Editore
Via Claudio Treves, 15/17
I – 20090 VIMODRONE (MI)
Tel. +39 02 27301126
Fax +39 02 27301454
E-mail: info@giorgionadaeditore.it
http: www.giorgionadaeditore.it

The catalogue of Giorgio Nada Editore publications is available on request at the above address.

Racing Lancias
ISBN: 88-7911-236-8

CONTENTS

- **Introduction** — 7
- **Fulvia Rallye HF 1.6** — 8
- **Stratos** — 24
- **037** — 40
- **Delta S4** — 58
- **Delta 4WD** — 76
- **Delta Integrale 16V** — 92
- **Delta Safari** — 104
- **D 50** — 116
- **D 25** — 134
- **F&M Special** — 148
- **Montecarlo** — 160
- **LC2** — 174

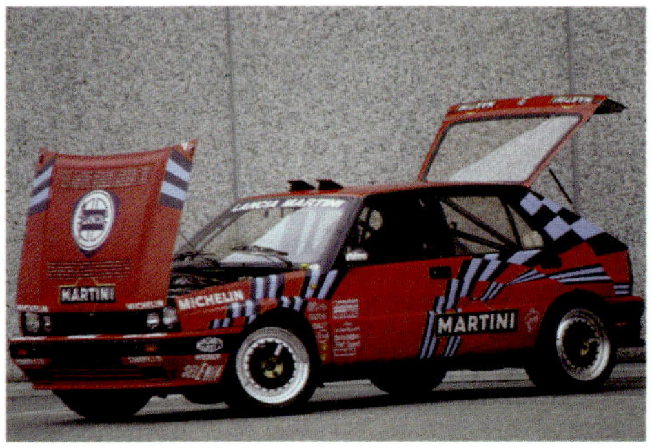
MARTINI
MICHELIN
MARTINI

Lancia and racing: a name, a word that is part of the motorcar's history. Almost half a century of Italian technology's sporting success and achievement in racing. From the D 50, the lone Formula One Lancia which, with its strange destiny, only conquered the world championship after being given to Ferrari, to the triumphant Delta, which won so much in world championship rallying. In this book, we have brought together some of the most beautiful and representative racing cars produced in Turin from the Fifties until today, featuring each model at the height of its technological development: the maximum evolution of the species. The cars represented here are those which were at the end of their respective chains of development. So that, although not wallowing in trophies like some of its stable mates in this book, the D 25 was included because it was the pinnacle of Lancia sports car evolution in the glorious Fifties: in much the same way, the extremely powerful LC2 was the "top" Lancia of the Eighties. Thanks, too, to a series of spectacular pictures, the stories of the 12 stars in this book are told in a creative as well as textually profound way: this approach helps to transmit what it was really like to be aboard these stupendous thoroughbreds as they generated their exceptional speed. Detailed technical specifications accompanied by a section in which the cars are shown racing at the time in which they were winning closes the review, a spectacular summa cum laude of Lancia's racing history: the history of a company which, it is hoped, will one day return to competition.

Giancarlo Reggiani

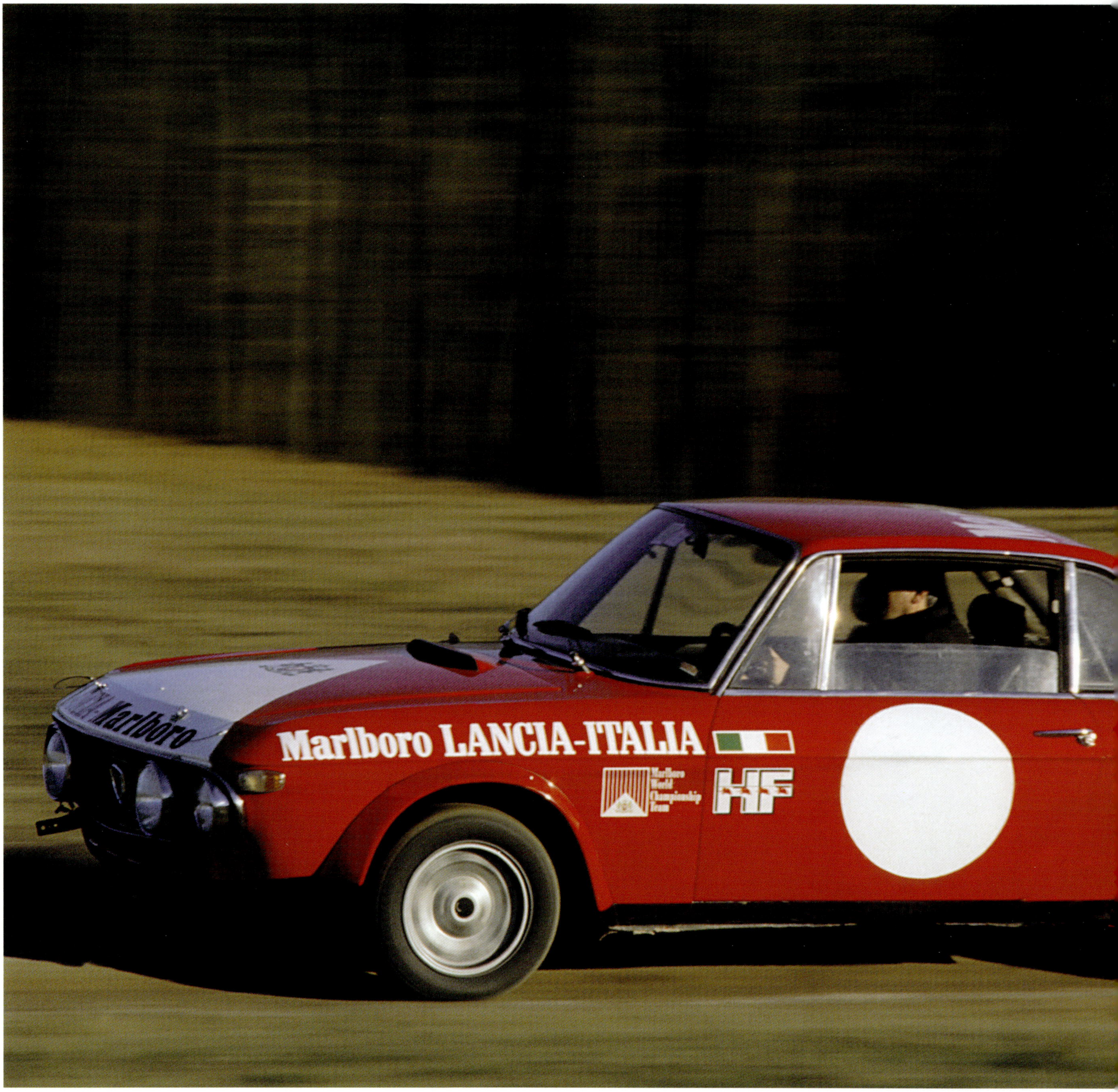
Marlboro
Marlboro LANCIA-ITALIA
HF

FULVIA RALLYE HF 1.6

This little Lancia occupied the number one spot in the heart of every "Lancista": it was the last sporting expression of the model. The mythical HF 1.6 "Fanalone" (Italian for big headlight) achieved success in the complex world of international rallying where, after a rapid top-level apprenticeship, it beat all its opponents. This coupé of the House of Lancia, winner of the 1972 International Rally Championship for Makes, was born a road car way back in 1965. It obtained its CSAI (the governing body of Italian motor sport) competition homologation in 1967 and immediately went into battle on the world stage. The car's first two seasons were used to assess the opposition's potential and, during that phase, it still won the 1300cc class of the 1967 European Touring Car Championship, driven by Claudio Maglioli. And in 1969, when Lancia went rallying, Harry Kallstrom competed in a number of events with the HF 1.3 and won the European Rally Championship. The new Rallye HF 1.6, developed from the road-going model, started out with an advantage its predecessor never had: before production of the road car began, Lancia developed the new car with a sporting future in mind. The "Fanalone", as it was later called by enthusiasts because of its two large supplementary front lights, was a car conceived almost specifically to race. The first and most obvious confirmation of this was, indeed, up front and easy to see: those two additional front lights flanking the radiator grill were especially designed to provide the drivers with better seeing power on the many special stages which were run at night. Among other things, it was this aggressive new front end look which generated tremendous public affection for the car and, as a consequence, the great commercial success of the road-going Rallye HF 1.6, for which the aesthetic variations all worked towards producing a racing image. For instance, the new matt-black wheel arch extensions widened the wings and enabled bigger alloy rims to be fitted (in line with CSAI regulations, of course) which, together with the appropriate tyres, produced better grip. Inside, too, the appearance of the instruments betrayed the car's promised performance, with exciting new maximums for the period: 220 km/h (137 mph) the speedometer and 10,000 rpm maxim the rev counter. The Fulvia HF 1.6 "Fanalone" was also introduced with different mechanics than the 1.3. The outdated four-speed gearbox gave way to a more modern five-speed unit. An easier-to-use and better-proportioned gear lever took the place of a hardly practical predecessor, which seemed kilometres long (it was not by chance that the first Fulvia coupé was nicknamed the "long lever".

The trademark big headlamps in all their impressive aggressiveness: a fascination that did not fade as the years passed.

Blue and yellow, the colours which have distinguished many sporting Lancias, were first carried into battle by the mythical D 24, which won the Carrera Panamericana: they were certainly a good omen for the engine of the HF.

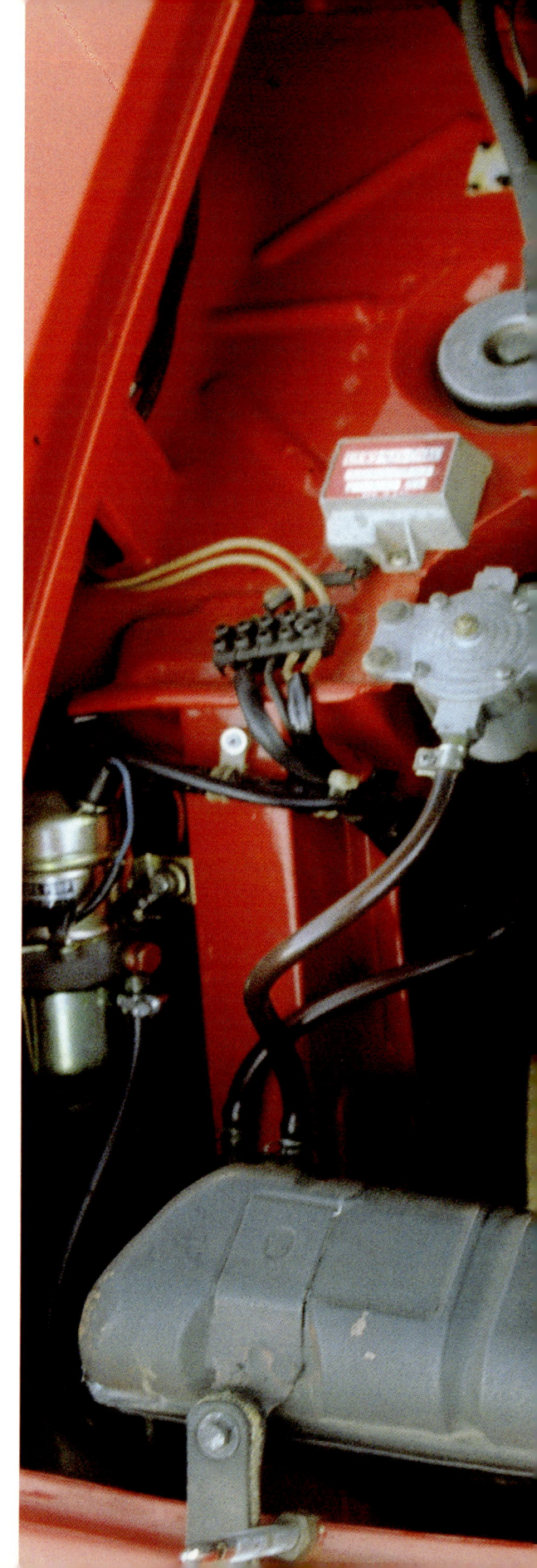

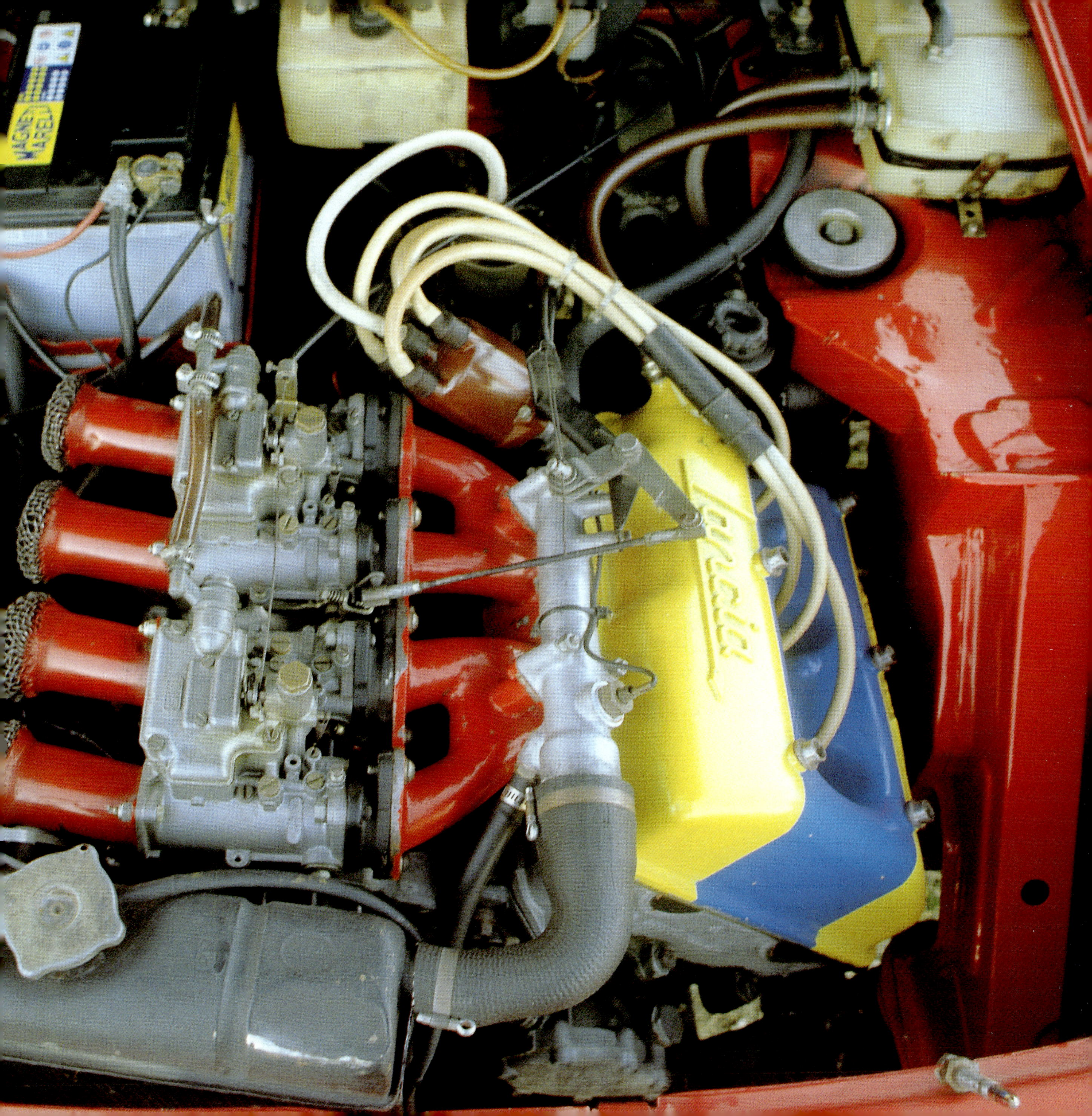
Lancia

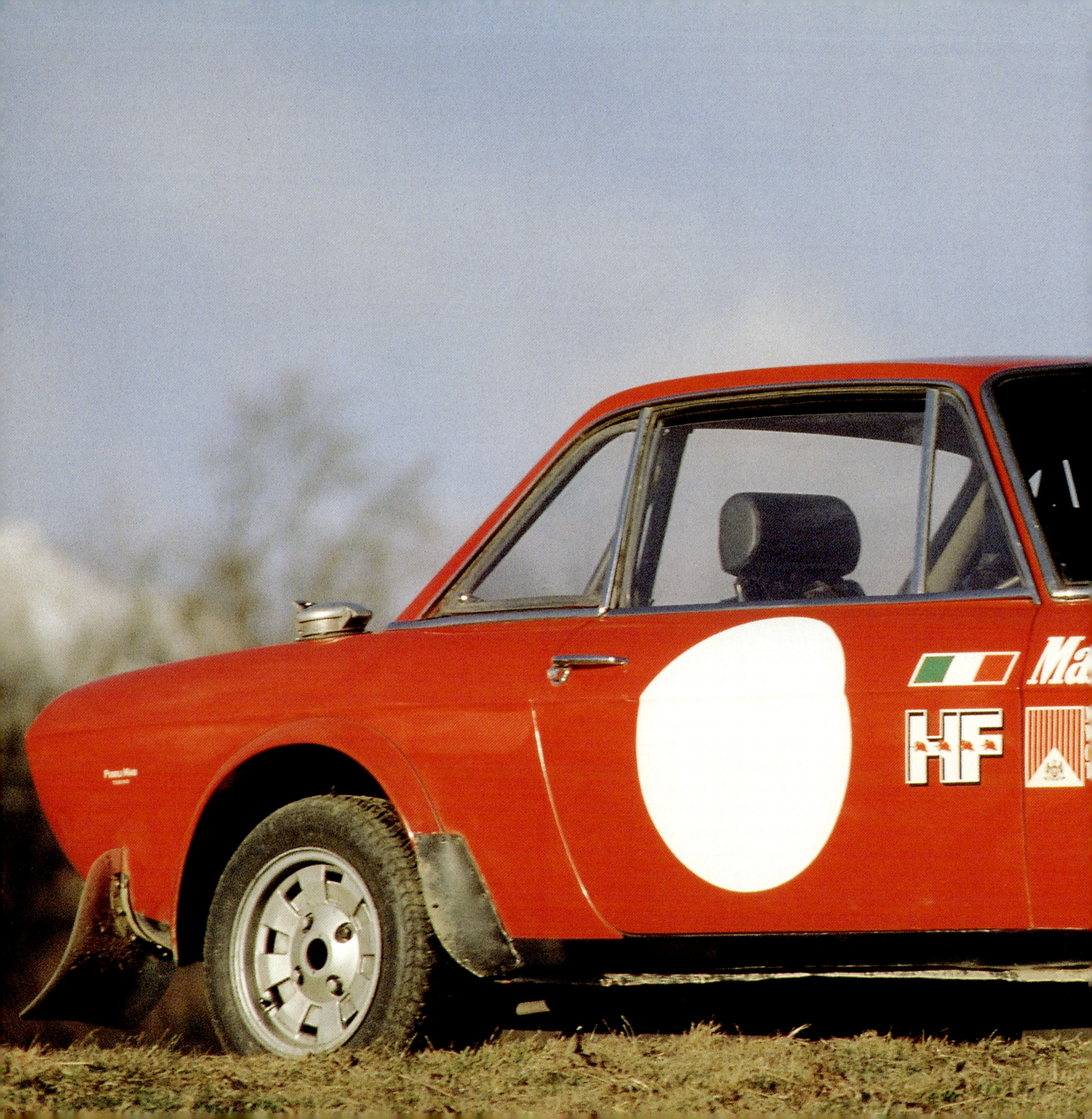
HF

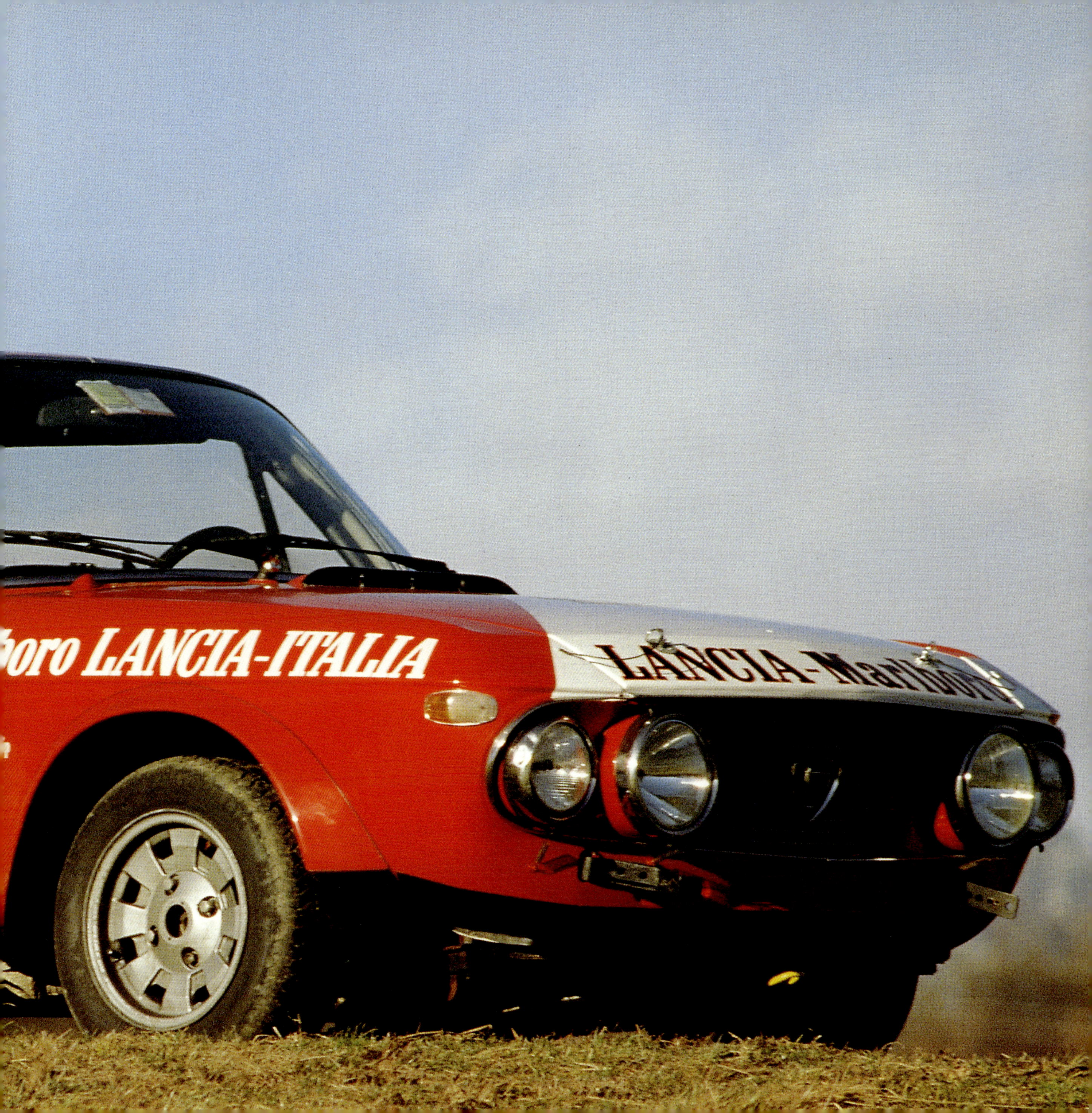
LANCIA-ITALIA
LANCIA-

Such mechanical evolution – provided it was, obviously, functional and of productive use on the other models in the range – gave a clear indication of the Turin manufacturer's real intentions: Lancia was to take to the rally arena with a most suitable and competitive car. Another technical improvement made to the HF 1.6 came from a one degree variation in the negative camber of the front wheels: that gave the new car better road holding, to which the new Cromodora alloy wheels in size 6J x 13 and HR speed-rated 175 mm section tyres also contributed. All these

The attractive light alloy Cromodora wheel fitted to an HF 1.6 added grit to the pretty coupé's appearance.

The characteristic nose of the HF 1.6 "Fanalone", which illuminates Lancia's sporting history for motor sport fans.

small but significant changes played their part in the commercial success of the second series Fulvia Coupé, but with the "Fanalone" they were there exclusively for competitive purposes. It should be said, however, that for operational cost reasons (at the time, Lancia was in a difficult financial situation and negotiations were taking place to sell the company to Fiat), the first 1000 Fulvia HF 1.6s were fitted with a gear-

15

box which, in reality, was just an evolution of the old four-speed: only the last 276 cars out of a total build of 1,278 adopted the new gearbox group developed for all top-of-the-range Lancias. The "Fanalone" had a completely new V4 1,584 cc engine, apart from a few items shared with the "old" 1300, among them the timing chain and tappet cover. The road going version of the 1.6 generated 115-horse power but, with its best sporting customers in mind, Lancia immediately put into production an elaboration kit (as it is called today!) which increased the car's power to 132 hp at 6600 rpm, with a maximum torque of 16.5 kg/m at the same rpm. So the competition history of the Fulvia HF 1.6 Rallye was developed from a good, concrete starting point to achieve its well-known results. Even though it was born at a time when Lancia still did not belong to Fiat, the HF "Fanalone" played a highly important role in the sports activity of the Group, because it was the first Lancia able to attract a major sponsor and significant finance to the world of rallying. The Marlboro livery, which first appeared on the Fulvia HF at the 1972 San Remo Rally won by Ballestrieri/Bernacchini, also ushered in a new era of sponsorship in the romantic (up to that point) world of road racing. The multitude of successes achieved by the little Lancia coupé that glorious year probably convinced several other would-be sponsors interested in promoting their image that international rallying could be a good investment. It was also in that mythical year that the Fulvia won seven times and achieved podium finishes which swung the spotlight firmly onto one of its drivers, a certain Sandro Munari. The previous year, he had already begun to make his name in the Lancia Rallye HF 1.6 and became synonymous with some of the Turin company's great rally successes, winning the 1977 FIA Drivers' Cup at the wheel of the Stratos. From 1969 to 1971, all the works racing cars were prepared in the Biella workshop of Claudio Maglioli, who was also responsible for development, testing, and racing in speed tests; these "special" Fulvias numbered 17 in total and in their final phase of evolution put out something like 158 hp at 7,500 rpm, with a maximum torque of 20 k/gm at 6,600 rpm. As well as making the chassis more robust with the application of an anti-roll bar and dome bars, Maglioli's work consisted of squeezing the

A tail often seen by Lancia's opponents, as the little coupé ran off and left them to eat its dust.

Left, graphics which bring back the "romantic" past of great sporting battles, fought out as a protagonist.

The lock of the aluminium petrol tank cap was particularly curious: fear of sabotage?

17

maximum amount of horsepower from the "Fanalone's" engine, without compromising the car's reliability. Judging by the results, the alchemy was completely successful and permitted these hot Fulvias to compete for the World Championship for Makes for six years. The car also contributed to another Lancia championship victory in 1974, by helping the Beta Montecarlo and the newborn Stratos to accumulate the necessary points with which to win that year's world manufacturers' titles. So before leaving the world stage to her heirs, the HF shared the points she scored in an entire championship, showing the Stratos the way to a distinguished career in much the same way that a mother would help her daughter!

A zoom into the most characteristic part of the Fulvia HF: its nose wrote with style some of the history of international rallying.

Right, a shaft of light illuminates the bridge of command from which the world rally championship was dominated: just the few essential instruments to keep everything under control.

18

19

Marlboro LANCIA-ITALIA
Marlboro
World
Championship
Team
HF

Technical specification of the FULVIA RALLYE HF 1.6

ENGINE: V4 at 11.2°
ENGINE POSITION: front, longitudinal
CUBIC CAPACITY: 1584 cc
BORE AND STROKE: 82x75 mm
DISTRIBUTION: single overhead camshaft per cylinder bank
NUMBER OF VALVES: 2 per cylinder
COMPRESSION RATIO: 10.5:1
FUEL SYSTEM: 2 Solex DDHF or DDHF/1 twin-choke carburettor
IGNITION: single coil
COOLING SYSTEM: liquid (one front radiator)
MAXIMUM POWER: 158 hp at 7500 rpm
MAXIMUM TORQUE: 20 kg/m at 6600 rpm
CAR BODY: two-seater coupé, steel
CHASSIS: central load-bearing monocoque in reinforced sheet steel with front under-chassis for engine and suspension support
SUSPENSION: front independent, superimposed triangles, telescopic shock absorbers rear, rigid axle, half-elliptical springs, stabiliser bar.
TRANSMISSION: four-speed and reverse ZF gearbox, front-wheel drive
CLUTCH: dry mono-disc
BRAKES: drum front and rear
DIMENSIONS: length 3935 mm, width 1570 mm, height 1300 mm
WHEELBASE AND TRACK: 2330 mm – 1390 mm front, 1335 mm rear
TYRES: front and rear Michelin 175-13 X AS
DRY WEIGHT: 1170 kg
PERFORMANCE: 129 mph (207 km/h) with long gear ratios
ACCELERATION: 0 – 100 km/h in 8 seconds

Claudio Maglioli's HF cornering in different events: the Targa Florio, a speed race in Vienna and a touring car championship event on the parabolica at Monza.

At Monza with style: Claudio Maglioli on the parabolica in the Fulvia HF.

A symbolic picture: a Fulvia at Sebring with a banner of one of Lancia's future sponsors in the background.

The photographs on pages 22 and 23 appear by courtesy of Claudio Maglioli.

23

STRATOS

Stratospheric in the true sense of the word: this was a car born to win and with a name (the abbreviation of the Italian word stratosfera or stratosphere) adopted to underline its innovative content. With advanced mechanical technology of an almost centrally mounted, transverse engine and an extremely short wheelbase which ensured outstanding handling, a fundamental requirement in rallying, the Stratos made its debut on the international motor sport stage as the new pretender to the world rally crown. The "Stratos Project" comes from the noble origins of a six cylinder Ferrari engine and, in particular, from the marriage of the Maranello company with Fiat: that liaison generated the first Dino six cylinder production car in 1966 and three years later the 2400 cc which, suitably revised, went into the Lancia Stratos. In the road-going Stratos, that engine, derived conceptually from the one designed in 1956 by Enzo Ferrari's late son Dino, put out 192 hp at 7000 rpm, but with the most extreme evolution of the rally specification its power output reached 300/305 hp at 8500 rpm. The chassis of this sports coupé was a central monocoque with steel reinforcement and boxed tube construction front and rear to support the suspension and engine. The body, built completely of glass fibre, was designed by Bertone and vaguely resembled their Stratos O prototype, which was unveiled at the 1970 Turin Motor Show to an astonished public. In fact, the science fiction-looking car was so low that its windscreen was almost horizontal to the ground. And when the Bertone prototype made its debut at Lancia, people said it looked like a tapered torpedo on four wheels: driven by the de-

Alitalia
ELABORAZIONE MAGLIOLI-BIELLA-ITALY
Alitalia
LANCIA
LANCIA

signer's head of public relations, it entered the factory's courtyard by literally passing under the waist-high security bar! It was precisely this futuristic study in car design which had its impact on the then head of the new-born Lancia racing and commercial department, Cesare Fiorio, convincing him that the mobile torpedo could be a suitable basis of development which would create the heir to the Fulvia HF legacy in world championship rallying. In fact, it was the enthusiasm and unconditional support of Fiorio for the Stratos O which enabled him to convince engineer Piero Gobbato, then director general of Lancia, to quickly put 500 cars (the minimum number necessary for homologation in rallying's Group 4) into production: that is how the Stratos broke through the barrier of doubt and perplexity which the major part of Lancia's management had ex-

From any perspective, power is the word to best describe Planet Stratos.

A very sharp wedge: the car has a profile that suggests the blade of a chisel.

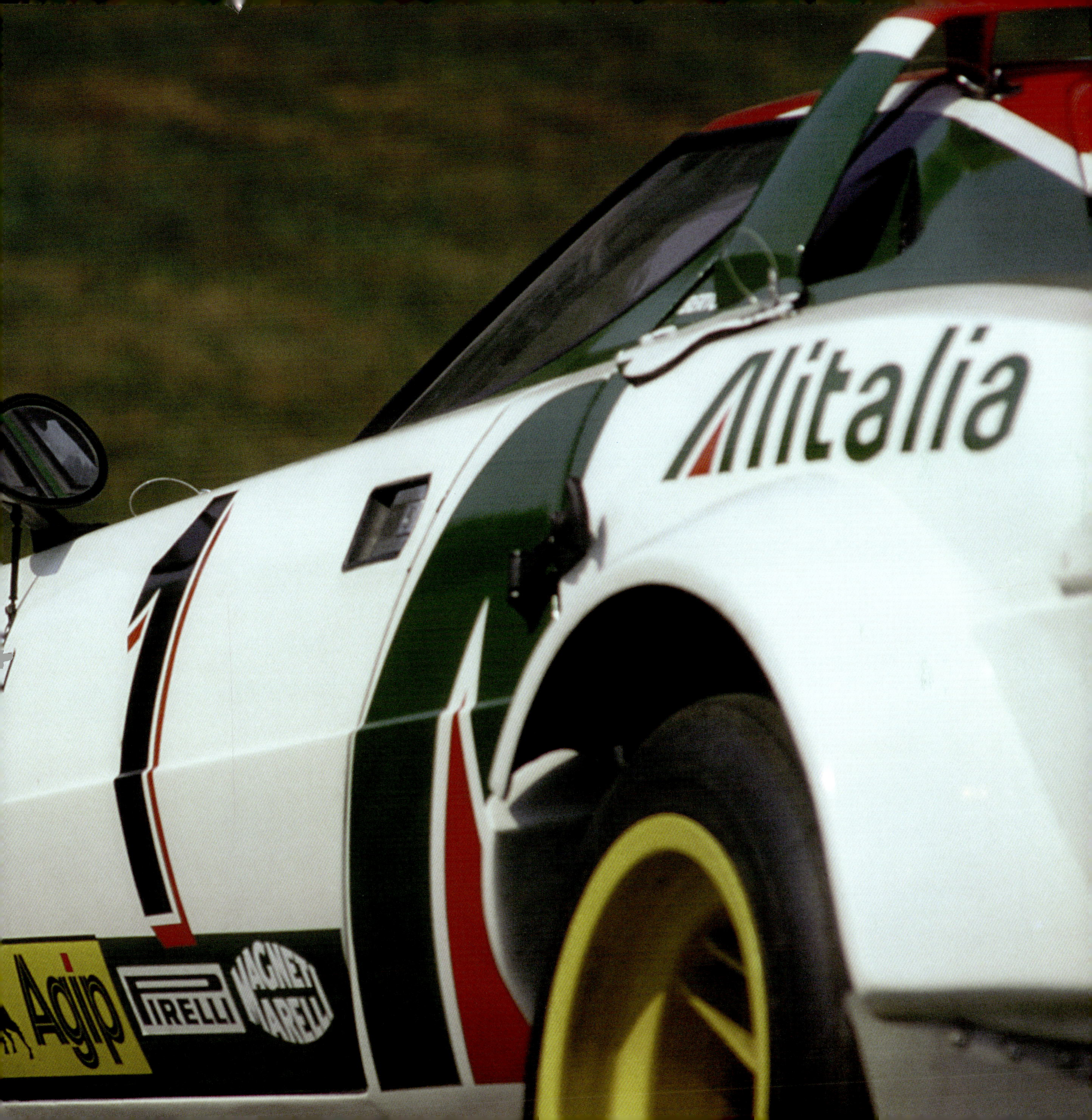
Alitalia
Agip
PIRELLI
MAGNETI MARELLI

pressed about the car. The new rally car's chassis was to be designed by specialists Giampaolo Dallara and Gianni Tonti, already well accustomed to the use of centrally mounted transverse engines. The body was to be by Nuccio Bertone, who had the young Marcello Gandini, who much later designed the Lamborghini Diablo among others, outline the essential features of this revolutionary sports coupé. A prototype of the car in its almost definitive form was unveiled at the 1971 Turin Motor Show and even then projected the shape which would become famous and, right from the start, threaten the supremacy of the heroine of the international rally championship at the time, the Renault Alpine A110. The tapered silhouette and compactness of this new Lancia, with its much-reduced wheelbase, immediately communicated the potential of this new "monster", which was to throw world championship rallying into such disarray. Its chassis, a central load-carrying monocoque structure, was conceived expressly for competition; it permitted rapid service and repair due to the car's two completely removable front and rear hoods and,

The very short wheelbase did not detract from the side panels, which still demonstrated an excellent equilibrium of shape.

Right, the convexity of the front wings was so pronounced that they greatly enlarged the silhouette of the car.

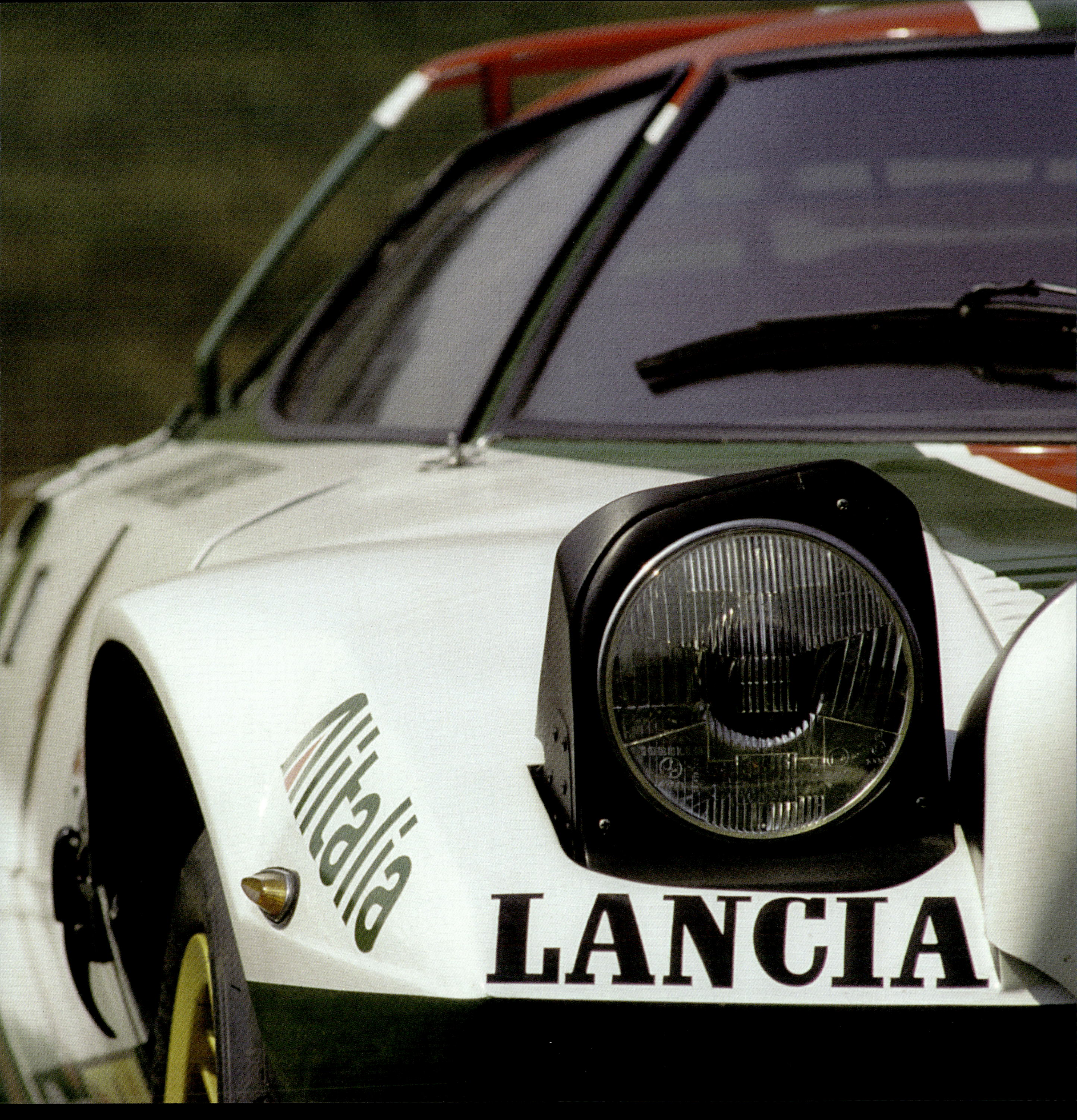
Alitalia
LANCIA

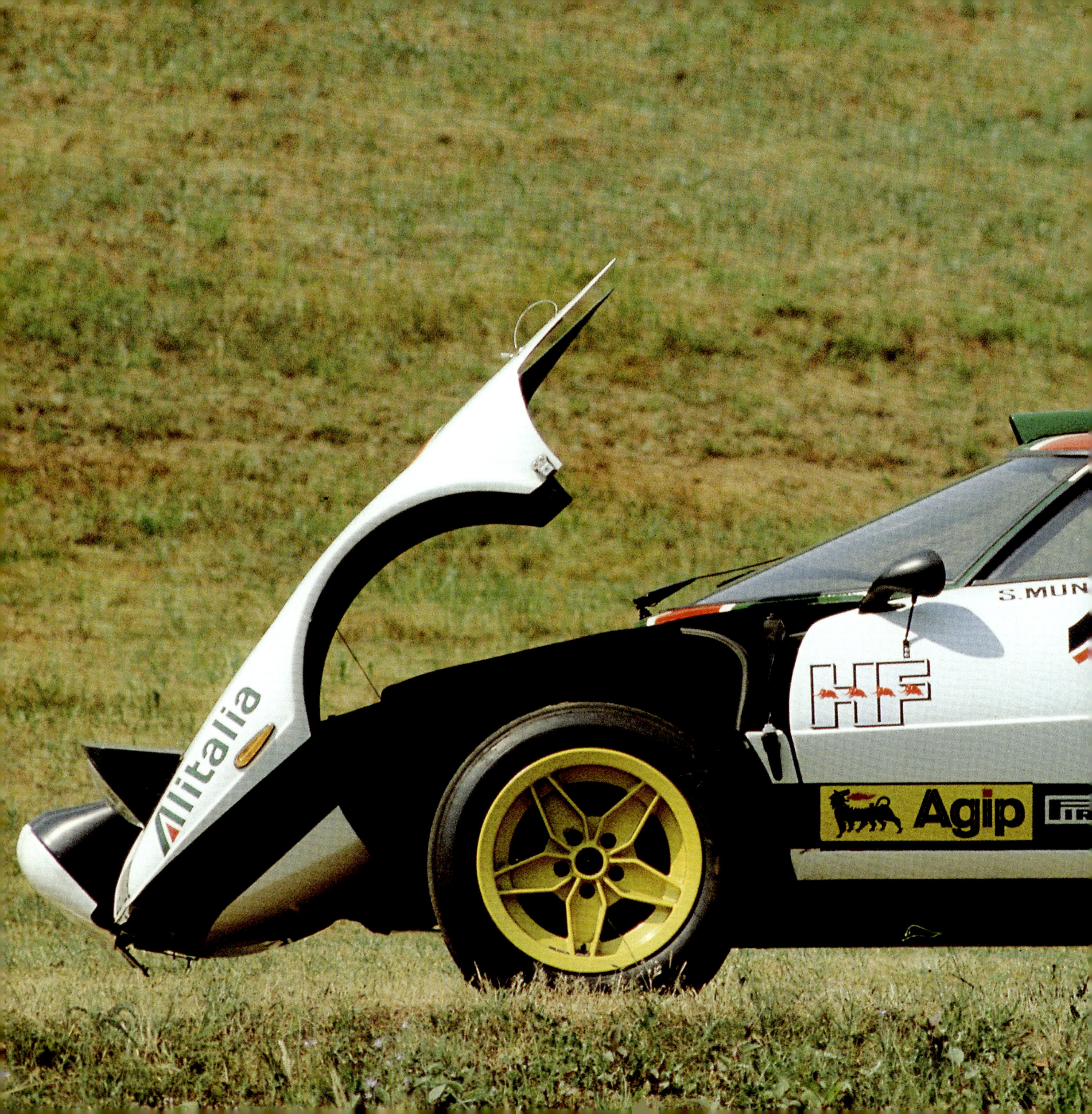
Alitalia
HF
Agip

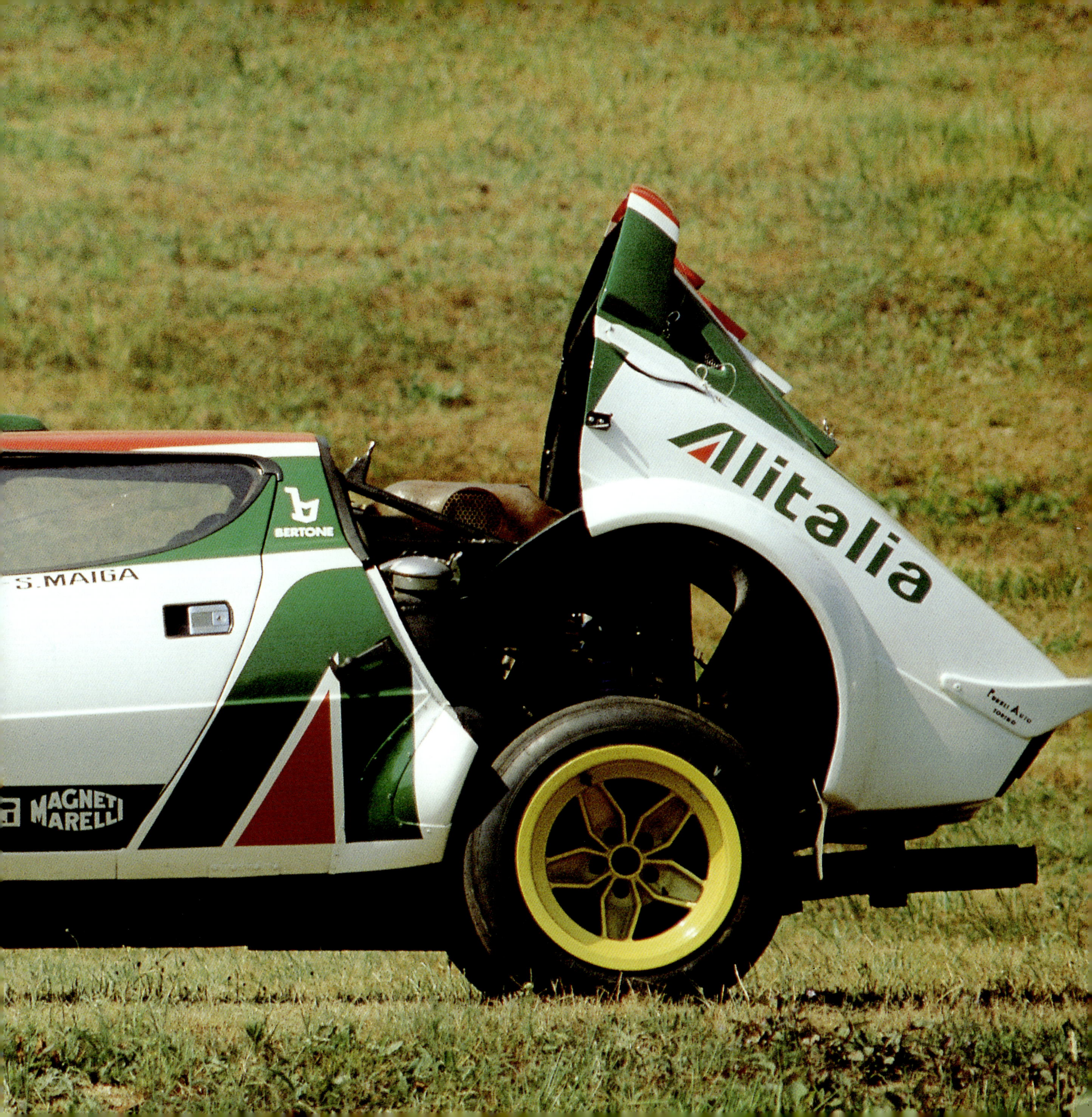
Alitalia
BERTONE
S.MAIGA
MAGNETI
MARELLI

therefore, notable access to all mechanical parts. Another small revolution ushered in by the Stratos project was the use of different size tyres for the front and rear axles: the larger width of the rears gave the new supercar an even more aggressive appearance but, above all else, considerably increased its road holding capacity. The only problem was there was a difference of opinion in Lancia between the technical design staff and the commercial sector over the type of tyre to adopt as a spare for the 500 road cars: in the end, a front tyre was mounted. The choice of engine was not such an easy matter, either: there were those who preferred the classical four cylinder, which was more in line with Lancia production; then there were those who opted (with success, as it turned out) for the higher performance and fractionalised six cylinder Ferrari Dino 2.4 and even those who had in mind two different engines, a four cylinder for the road-going version and a six cylinder for the rally car. The Dino supporters eventually won the day and the Stratos prototype making its debut at the 1971 Turin show did so with the 65° Ferrari V6 2418 cc engine. The road car power plant produced 192 hp at 7000 rpm, but by 1976 the rally version had evolved into a 24-valve unit, which put out 305 hp at 8500 rpm and put down 29 kg/m of torque at 6500 rpm. This jewel of a Lancia was prepared by Claudio Maglioli, one of the most enthusiastic supporters of the Stratos project, at his workshop in Biella, where he divined most of the works and non-works Stratos cars which competed so successfully on the special stages of the world. The car made its competitive debut driven by Sandro Munari in the 1972 Giro di Corsica, but retired with suspension problems. In fact, it took until 1973 for the revolutionary new Lancia to achieve its first victory: it won the Fire-

In the previous double-page spread the Stratos, stripped of its front and rear hoods, shows the splendour of its opposing ends.

Several details which characterised this sports coupé: the unusual yellow wheels, the round tail light encased in black, the much-inclined windscreen and door mirror, the rear wing, the front headlight raised and ready for use.

Left, the wing placed above the rear hood deviated the airflow, improving overall aerodynamics.

stone Rally in Spain driven by Munari and made its opponents eat its dust, also giving the world of rallying its first glimpse of Stratos ferocity. The car won its first world manufacturers' championship in 1974 with the two valves per cylinder engine which, at the end of its evolution cycle, generated 270 hp at 7800 rpm. A new, hotter version of the Stratos with many technical improvements was homologated and came out immediately after the 1975 Monte Carlo Rally: the new four valves per cylinder Dino-engined evolution car produced 300/305 hp at 8500 rpm and in this configuration won another two world manufacturers' championships in 1975 and 1976. After its triumph in the 1977 Monte Carlo Rally, the car's premature destiny was decided by Fiat Group company politics, which preferred to push the new-born 131 Abarth: the boxy Fiat was more representative of the company's production at the time and, therefore, more suited to be the Turin group's standard bearer. And that, sadly, is why a car which had shown all its competitors the way on the special stages of the world and beyond for most of the Seventies was denied the chance to continue in motor sport: it was the wrong shape. Claudio Maglioli said later that, at the time, he was developing an extreme version of the Stratos, using the eight-cylinder engine of the Ferrari 308 GTB. A 'no limits' beast of at least 400 hp to demonstrate that the Stratos still had considerable development potential. Unfortunately, however, Ferrari did not agree with the use of such a colossus in this way, so in 1978 Stratos was officially withdrawn from rallying, leaving the field clear for the new Fiat 131 Abarth. But the mesmeric Lancia, that child of the stratosphere, could not really complain: no-one could deprive it of its prestigious treasure trove of victories and world championships.

Opening the Stratos' bonnet, the six cylinder Dino could only be detected by its red rocker covers, and even they were hidden by the large resin carburettor air intake duct. Space was at a premium in the Stratos' cockpit, but all controls were perfectly aligned: for the period, command centre had the look of a spacecraft's interior.

TRIPMASTER
halda
1/2
4/4
FARI SUPPL.
FARI EMERG.
REOST.
CRONO — NOTE
S POMPE BENZ. D
LUCI RETRO
VENT. RISC.
POST. ANT.
ONTATTO
AVVIAM.

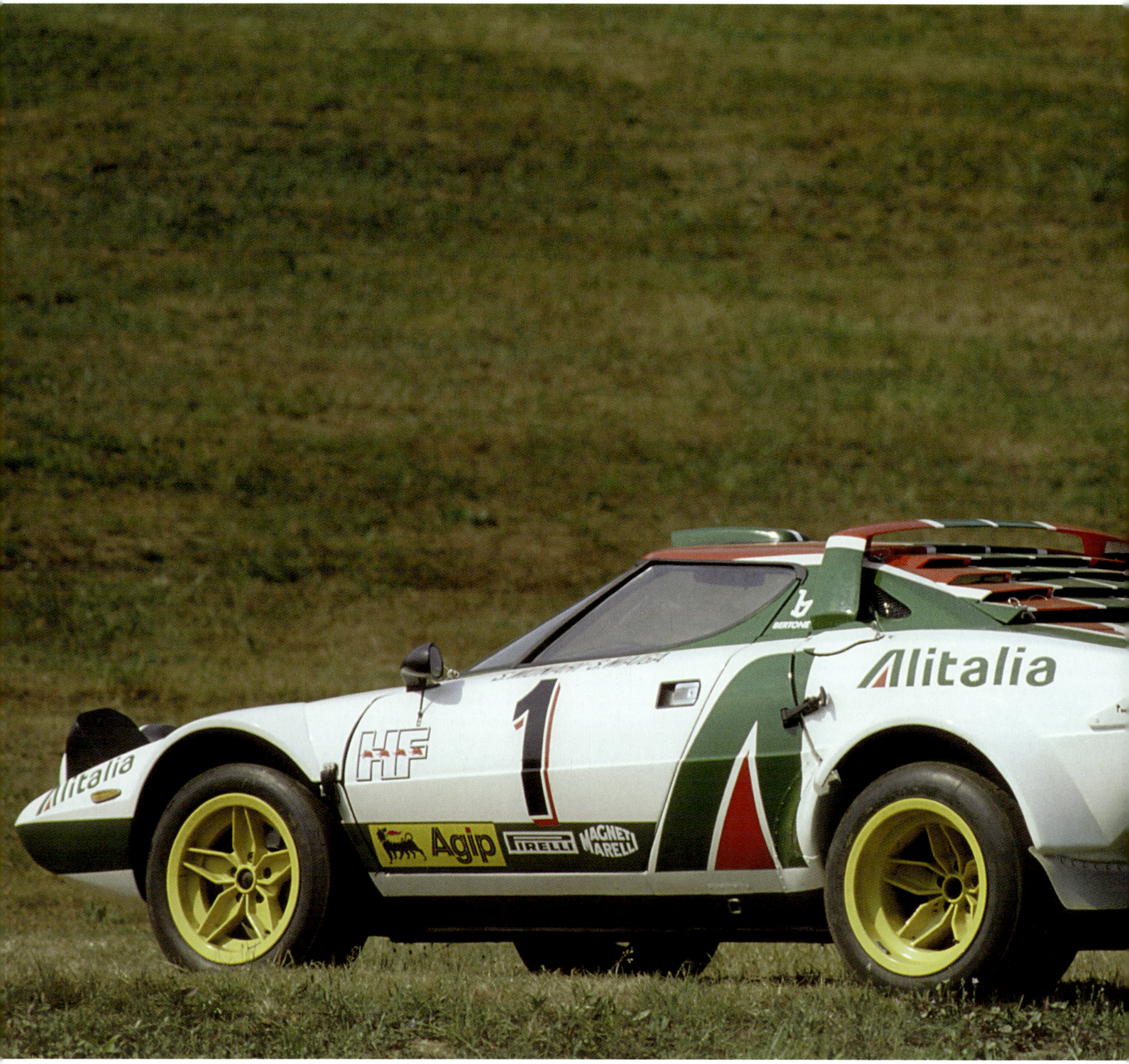
Alitalia
1
HF
Agip
PIRELLI
MAGNETI MARELLI
Alitalia

Technical specification of the STRATOS 24 VALVE

ENGINE: V6 at 65°
ENGINE POSITION: centre rear, transversal
CUBIC CAPACITY: 2418 cc
BORE AND STROKE: 92.50X60 mm
DISTRIBUTION: two overhead camshafts per cylinder bank
NUMBER OF VALVES: 4 per cylinder
COMPRESSION RATIO: 9:1
FUEL SYSTEM: 3 Weber twin choke 48 DCF carburettors
IGNITION: Dinoplex electronic
COOLING: liquid (one front radiator)
MAXIMUM POWER OUTPUT: 305 hp at 8500 rpm
MAXIMUM TORQUE: 29 kg/m at 6500 rpm
BODY: two-seater coupé in glass fibre
CHASSIS: central monocoque in sheet metal reinforced with steel tubes and a structure in rectangular steel tubing supporting suspension and engine
SUSPENSION: independent all round, transversal four-sided front and transversal triangles rear, front struts reacting to stabiliser bars, telescopic shock absorbers and helicoidal springs.
TRANSMISSION: 5 speed plus reverse ZF gearbox, rear-wheel drive
CLUTCH: single dry disc
BRAKES: self-ventilating discs front and rear
DIMENSIONS: length 3710 mm, width 1850 mm, height 1170 mm
WHEELBASE AND TRACK: 2180 mm; 1430 mm front, 1460 mm rear
TYRES: front Michelin 17/63VR15, rear Michelin 23/62VR15
DRY WEIGHT: 890 kg
PERFORMANCE: maximum speed from 90-137 mph (152 to 220 km/h), depending on gear ratios
ACCELERATION: 0 – 100 km/h in 4.1 seconds using short gear ratios

Top and bottom: Two private Stratos competing in the 1979 Rally of Monza. Even non-works cars in the Italian and European championships proved competitive, scoring a number of victories.

The Alitalia Stratos of Sandro Munari-Mario Mannucci, the car featured in this chapter's photographs, winning the 1977 Monte Carlo Rally.

Tyres with sharp "claws" fitted to the Munari-Mannucci Stratos on the ice of the 1975 Monte Carlo Rally.

Photograph by courtesy of the Lancia Historic Archive.

Photograph by courtesy of the Lancia Historic Archive.

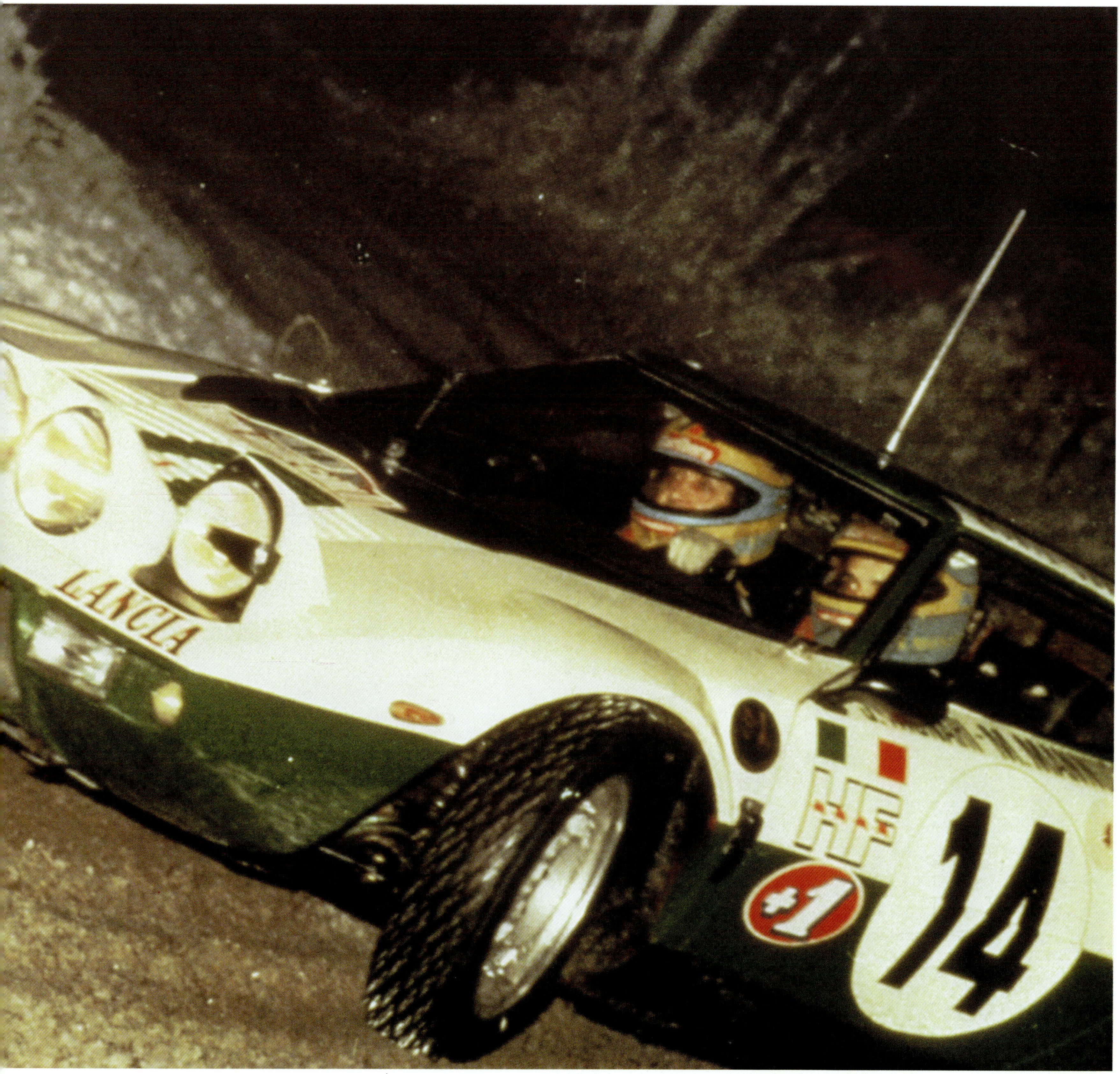
LANCIA
HF
14

037

Attilio Bettega loved the 037, knew it well and was able to completely dominate it, taking the sleek coupé to the limit as few others could: he once told me that driving the 960 kg 037 with 310 hp going out through the rear wheels took a lot of guts but, more than anything else, great concentration. When Bettega and I met at San Marino to create together a series of very special photographs with my somewhat strange camera, which "spied" on the driver from its attachment on the front of the car, Bettega was enthusiastic about the 037 and happy to be able to drive it. But he confided that, even then, they were reaching the limit: he said driving such a car on unmade special stages could soon be beyond human endeavour. We know, unfortunately, what was the epilogue to the Group B scramble and the destiny of poor Bettega, but the 037 remains a fascinating milestone in the history of world championship rallying and, perhaps, the last car in the category which could still be controlled with comparative ease by a handful of drivers. My first meeting with the 037 was at its birthplace, the Abarth racing department in Corso Marche, Turin. I saw the car born and assembled. The naked road car monocoques waiting to be transformed into the rallying supercars we know today: even that first encounter commanded respect and subjection. I was in San Marino to make a photographic dream come true: fit a camera, its timer already activated, onto the nose of this technological masterpiece of the House of Lancia. I was met by a willing Giorgio Pianta, the "father" of the 037, who guided the step by step development of this promising new-born, helped by the technicians who worked on the car and knew its every secret. They were all confident of their new Lancia's competitiveness (even if things did not go too well at the beginning) and the atmosphere was one of an enthusiastic atelier of technology. My proposal to take those special pictures coincided with the period of maximum development of that beautiful Group B car and for this reason,

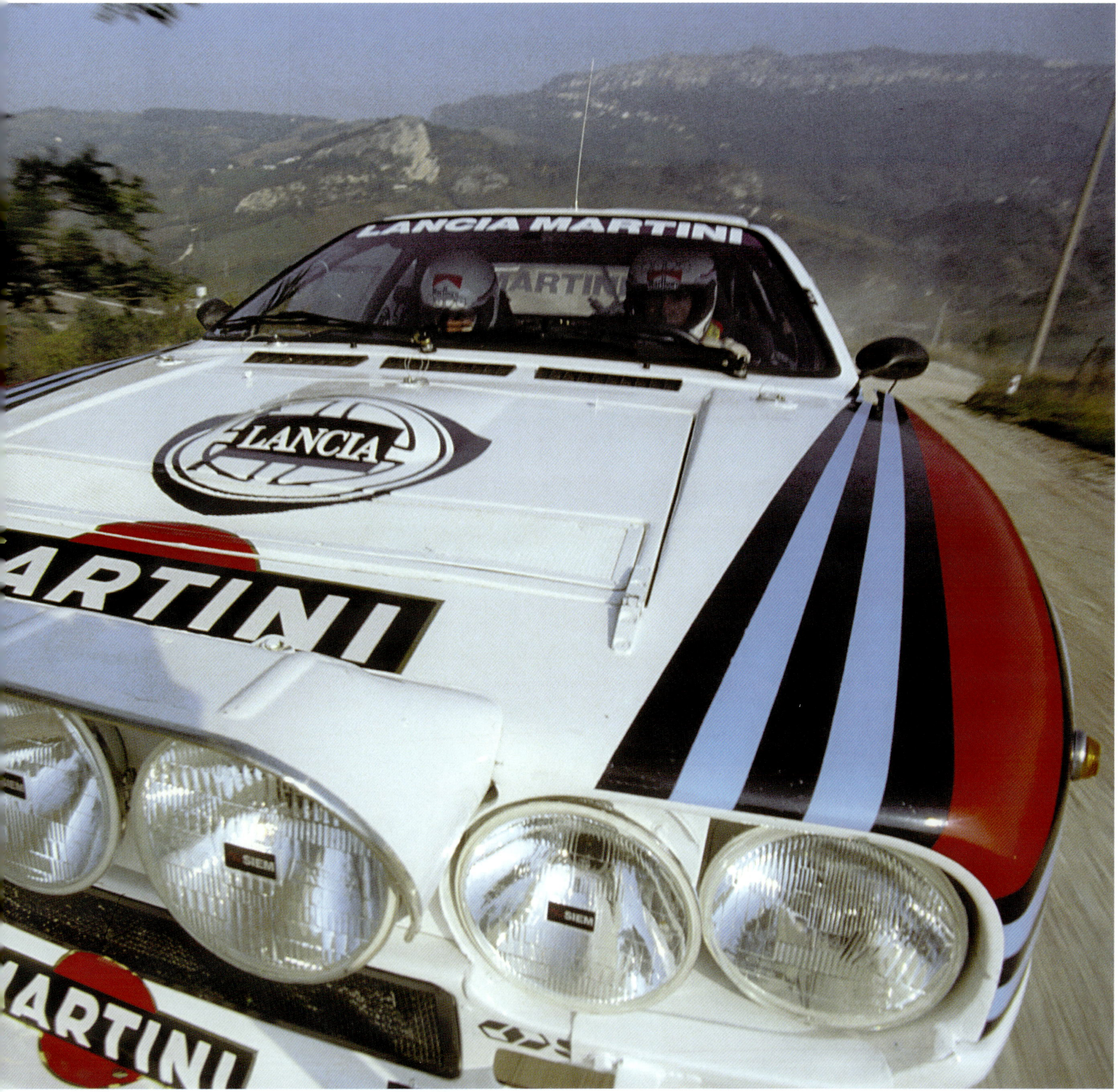
LANCIA MARTINI
LANCIA
MARTINI
SIEM
SIEM
MARTINI

LANCIA
MAGNETI MARELLI
speedline
brembo
BILSTEIN
Savara
TRW Sabelt
FERODO
OLIO FIAT
VS
PIRELLI
MARTINI
PIRELLI

too, I was amazed at the seriousness with which my project was taken into consideration. While Abarth was hard at work trying to win the world championship, someone there still had the time and will to listen to me and to make a support which, fitted to the front of their new car, would keep my camera rock steady and enable me to shoot some exceptional photographs, among them the one which appears at the beginning of this chapter. They told me straight away that we would be able to work better and without interruption at San Marino, rather than during the San Remo Rally, and they promised me that, before beginning their test programme, the specially-built bonnet with my camera support would be fitted to Attilio Bettega's 037. And so it was: on 30 October, 1984, Bettega saw his car arrive with a metal cantilever about a metre long

Like a peacock showing its plumes, the 037 with front and back hoods open to create quite a spectacle.

At speed, the big rear spoiler evened out the weight between the two axles.

43

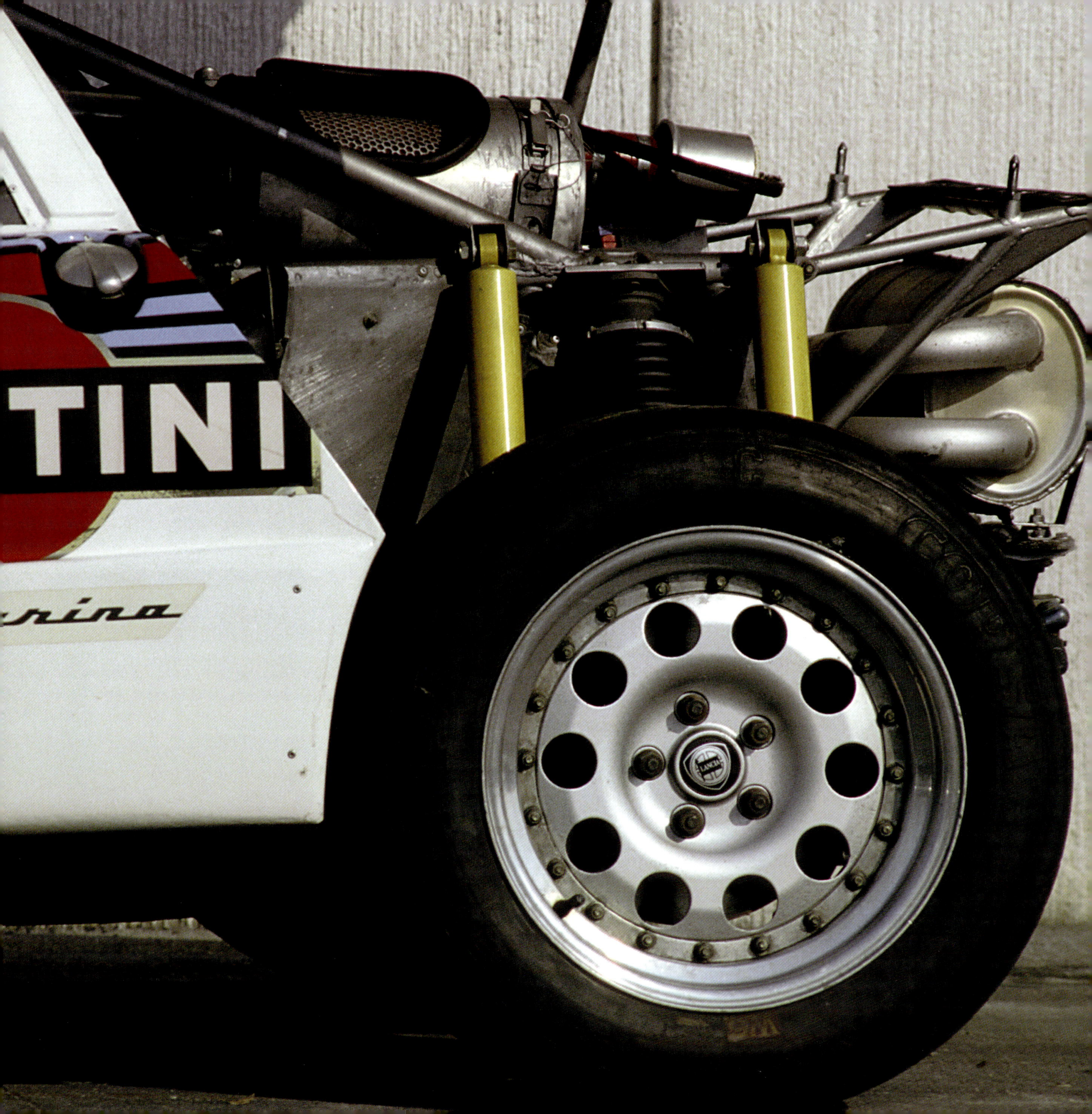
TINI

sticking out of its nose and my camera fitted to the top of that. With some perplexity but great willingness to co-operate, which was so typical of the man, Attilio went out on the first San Marino special stage with this device mounted on the car he loved so much.

But to re-trace the history of the 037's evolution it is necessary to go back to 1982 when Lancia put the Rally, purpose-built to bring the 037 to life and have it homologated for Group B, into production. The first 150 cars (a total of 420 were built for road and rally use) of this 037 road "matrix" were sold on paper in the wake of the enthusiasm that those in the know expressed at the time for this new Lancia. And their enthusiasm was not misplaced. The 037 put out 105 hp more than the road version and weighed 210 kg less. All of which gave it breath-taking performance and handling plus the ability to put down safely all that available horsepower through just two driven wheels, compared to some of its rivals with four-wheel drive. The 037 which, in effect, substituted the fierce Fiat 131 Abarth

A perfect mechanical sculpture: the gearbox and exhaust pipes nestle threateningly in the car's tail.

The large dismountable rim is unable to completely hide the huge rear shock absorbers.

MAGNETI MARELLI
speedline
brembo
BILSTEIN
Savara
TRW Sabelt
FERODO
OLIO
VS FIAT

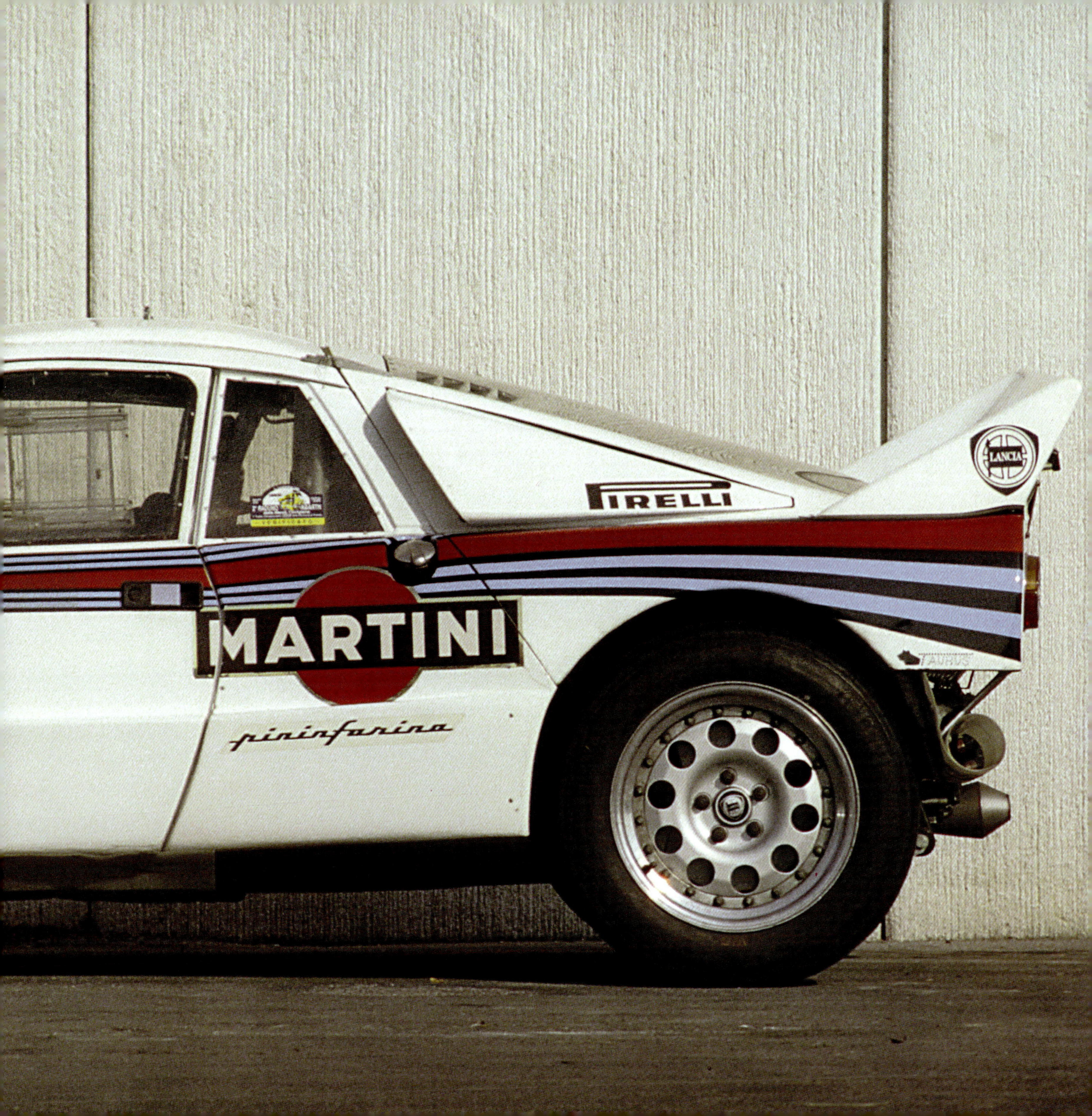
PIRELLI
LANCIA
MARTINI
pininfarina

monocoque structure with front and rear sub-frames and an extremely light Kevlar skin produced exceptional robustness but with minimum weight. The suspension units had aluminium bodied shock absorbers (steel for the rough, unmade special stages) linear bi-springs and double telescopic shock absorbers for the rear end. The distribution characteristics typical of volumetric supercharging gave the 037 fantastic driveability, in particular because of the fluidity of its four cylinder, four valves per cylinder 1995 cc engine, which produced a torque rate of 30.5 kg/m at 5500 rpm. By 1984, the 037 had been further developed into the Evolution 1, a faster version with a 2111 cc engine that delivered 325 hp at

The coloured stripes of the 037's sponsor seem to radiate from the two headlamps.

Right: The attractive flanks of the 037 did not detract from the muscles of this sports coupé.

The aluminium fuel tank cap was recessed into the car's side.

These vents allow the engine to breathe better.

as the Group's new sporting image, became the rival par excellence of the Audi Quattro which, until then, had dominated the world rally championship. At first, perhaps, some people underestimated a little the potential of the unborn two-wheel drive Lancia, but that was a serious mistake: it did not take more than a few rallies for the car to earn and command the respect of its opponents. Driven in 1983 by the highly talented team of Walter Rohrl, Markku Alen and Attilio Bettega, the 037 won the World Rally Championship for Makes, the most coveted title for a car manufacturer. This extraordinary child of the turbo era technology was also packed with state-of-the-art chassis innovations. The central

8000 rpm, 15 hp more than its predecessor. The Lancia sports coupé, however, was not only a rampaging rally phenomenon, it was also an outstanding looking car: its powerful muscles were cleverly blended into the elegant lines of the magnificent Pininfarina body which did not detract from the car's performance and allowed its beauty to emerge with great class. Everything had been carefully calculated to ensure that the 037 wrapped itself around its crew: from the driving position, which was all but perfect, to the two bumps in the roof to give the drivers and their helmets more headroom. Getting in and out of the 037's cockpit, as I did during a photographic shoot, is an unforgettable experience for a race fan: space is reduced to a minimum (I had to wrestle with my camera and flash) but everything is in exactly the right place. As I was able to verify, the driving position is really perfect and enables the pilot to move at supersonic speed between the gear lever, accelerator pedal, footbrake and clutch, although the latter is little used during a rally. On a special stage, all these movements must be made quickly so as to be competitive; as Giorgio Pianta has always maintained, a good sitting position allows the driver to earn precious fractions of a second (even, perhaps, seconds in the right circumstances) without having to increase engine power.

The bare essentials of the cockpit emphasise the high quality of materials used to create the 037.

The powerhouse of the 037, home of high technology, which has its special kind of beauty.

A simple round light on such a noble car takes us back to the past.

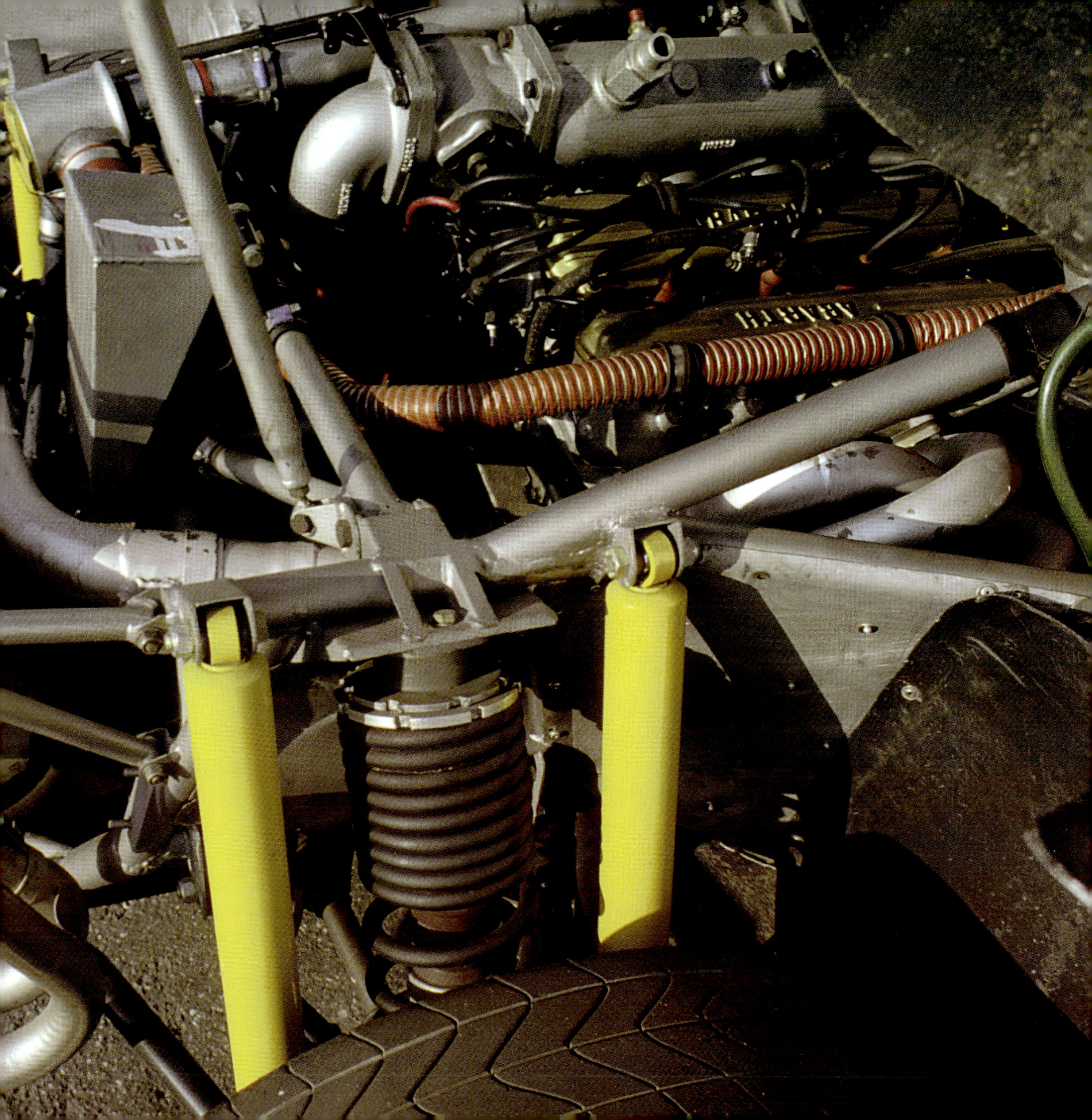

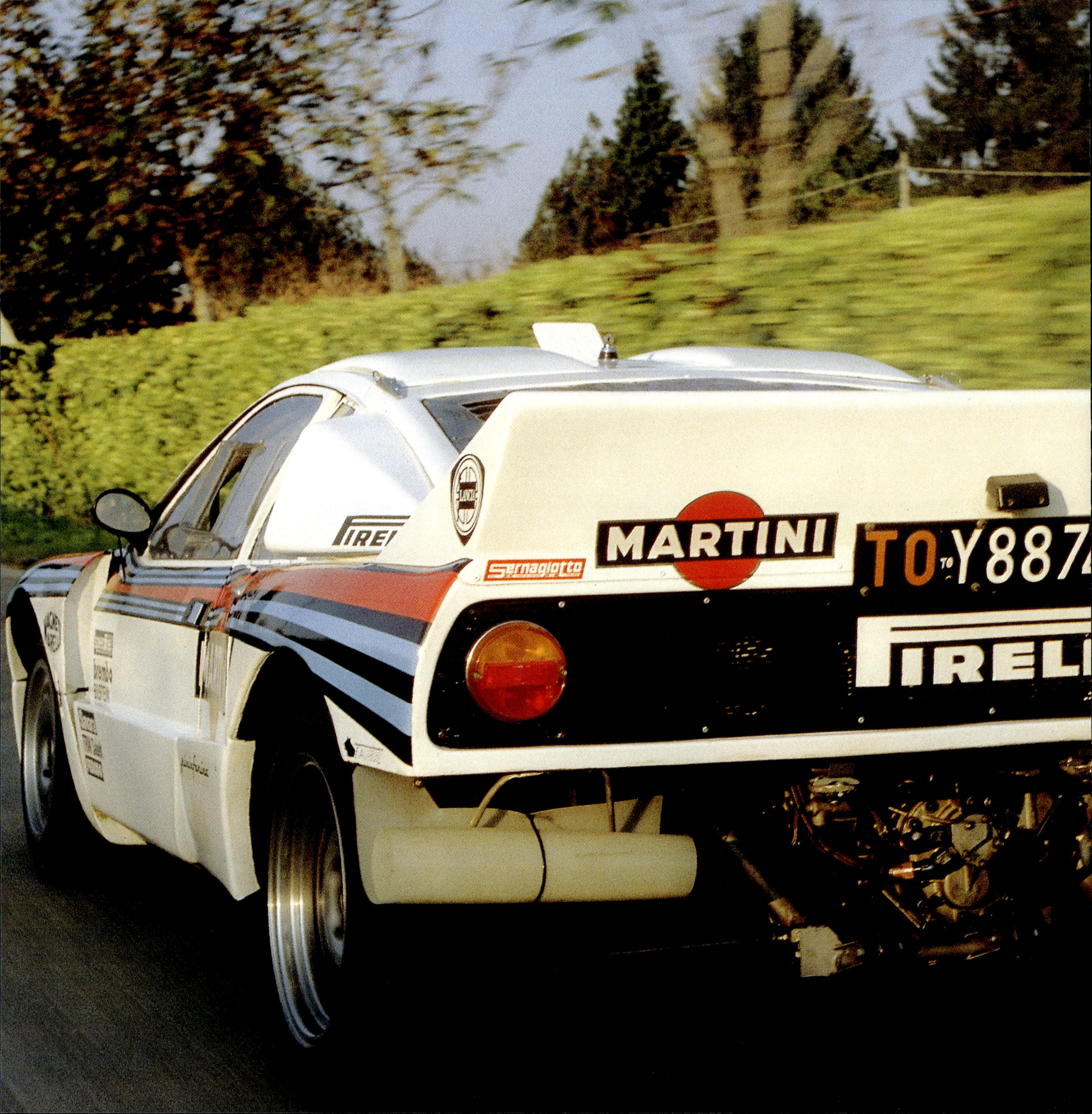
MARTINI
Sernagiotto

Technical specification of the 037

ENGINE: four cylinders in line
ENGINE POSITION: rear, central, longitudinal
CUBIC CAPACITY: 1998 cc (1984 version 2111 cc)
BORE AND STROKE: 84X90 mm (1984 version 85X93 mm)
DISTRIBUTION: two belt-driven overhead camshafts
NUMBER OF VALVES: four per cylinder
COMPRESSION RATIO: 9:1
FUEL SYSTEM: twin-choke Weber carburettors and volumetric supercharger (1984 version of the Kugelfisher indirect electronic fuel injection)
IGNITION: Marelli electronic I.A.W.
COOLING: liquid, one front radiator
MAXIMUM POWER: 310 hp at 8000 rpm (1984 version 325 hp)
MAXIMUM TORQUE: 30.5 kg/m at 5500 rpm (1984 version 33 kg/m at 5500 rpm)
BODY: two-seater coupé in Kevlar with the canopy in carbon fibre
CHASSIS: central load-carrying monocoque with front and back under chassis
SUSPENSION: independent all-round, front stabiliser bar, double rear shock absorbers
TRANSMISSION: five-speed gearbox with reverse, rear-wheel drive
CLUTCH: single dry disc
BRAKES: self-ventilating discs front and rear
DIMENSIONS: length 3915 mm, width 1850 mm, height 1245 mm
WHEELBASE AND TRACK: 2440 mm; front 1508 mm, rear 1490 mm
TYRES: front 210/595-15, rear 265/40-16
WEIGHT (DRY): 970 kg (unmade surface version 985 kg)
PERFORMANCE: maximum speed 109 mph (176 km/h) with short gear ratios
ACCELERATION: 0-400 metres in 12.2 seconds

Pictures of the 037s crewed by Walter Rohrl-Christian Geistdorfer and Markku Alen-Illka Kivimaki on one of the rough, unmade stages of the 1983 Rally of San Remo.

Like many of the greatest rally cars, the 037 lived a lot of its competitive life on opposite lock, particularly due to its exuberant power output all of which had to be put down by the rear wheels.

A 'virtual' zoom: the 037 opposite locking in spectacular fashion on the 1983 Rally of San Remo in the talented hands of (top to bottom) Adartico Vudafieri, Fabrizio Tabaton and, in the Lancia Martini racing team's official colours, the late Attilio Bettega.

A professional secret revealed. This (above) is how the photographs at the beginning and end of this chapter were taken: the camera is aboard Bettega's 037.

The Bettega/Perissinot 037 flies in the half light (right) while practising for the San Marino.

Close-up (below) of the camera mounted on a stable support specially made by Abarth for Giancarlo Reggiani and fitted to the front body cowling Bettega's 037.

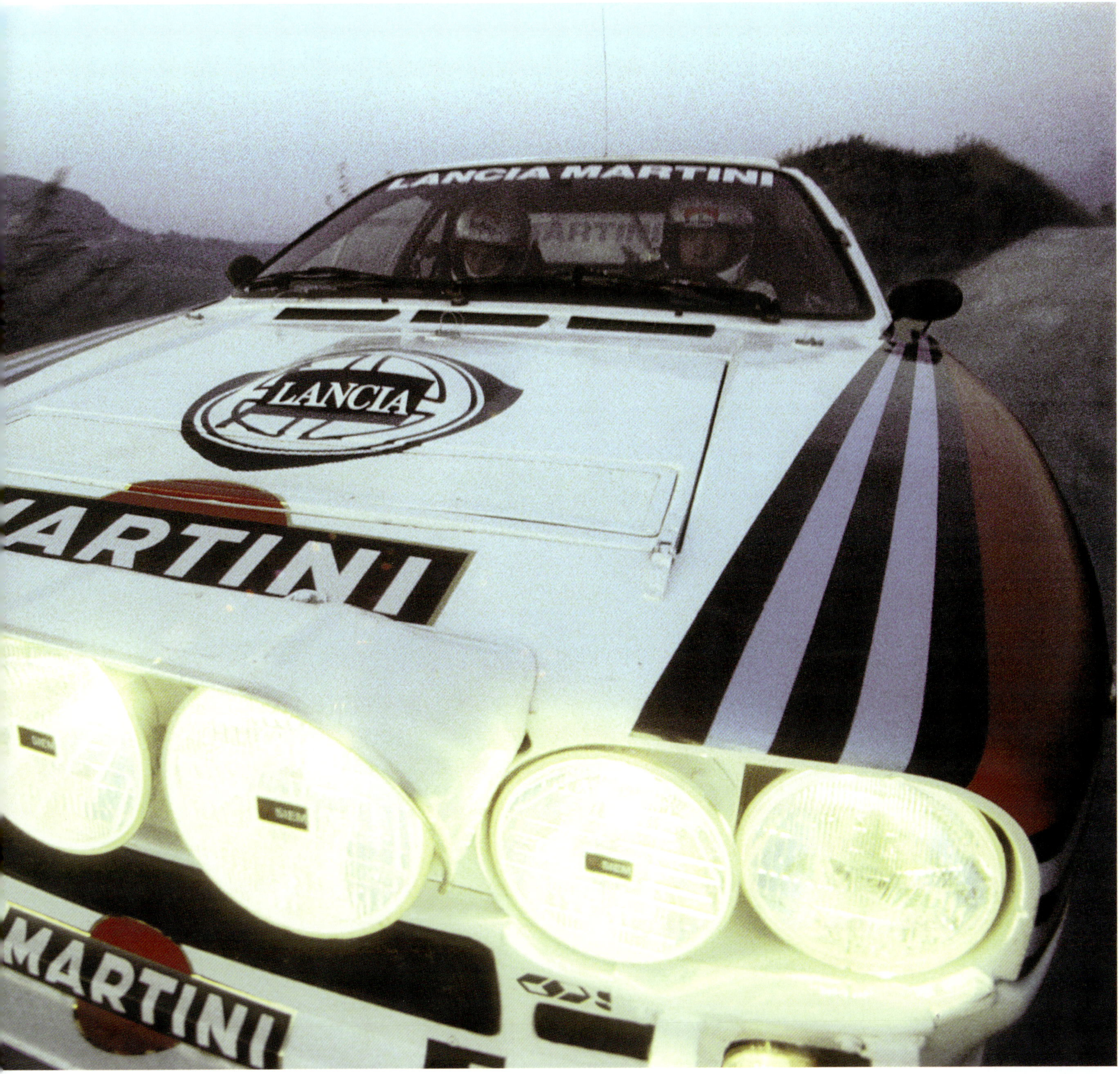
LANCIA MARTINI
LANCIA
MARTINI
MARTINI

DELTA S4

The Delta S4 was to be Lancia's outright winner in Group B international rallying and it made its debut right on time to oppose the domination of its adversaries in the 1985 world rally championship. The car's immense potential became evident immediately: it won its first ever rally less than a month after being homologated (1 November, 1985). Henri Toivonen/Neil Wilson and Markku Alen/Illka Kivimaki took first and second places in the Britain's world championship RAC Rally. Not bad for first time out. And just in case some people thought that win was a flash in the pan, Toivonen's victory in the 1986 Monte Carlo Rally, the year's opener, cleared up all remaining doubts. A great car. But to arrive at that point, the S4 began its journey on the drawing board back in June, 1983, when the Fiat Group started to develop its first four-wheel drive car. The requirements were extremely precise, even categorical: beat Peugeot at its own game, a game initiated by Audi with the Quattro after which four-wheel drive had become an indispensable essential to being competitive. And that is how it was. All Lancia's technical staff involved in the project embarked on their first four-wheel drive enterprise and that is why it took so long to develop their competitive "monster". They also had to confront a number of functional problems linked to speed of servicing and repair, which is why they chose a tubular chassis instead of a monocoque. Three self-locking differentials were adopted, the central unit a Ferguson viscous coupling unit. Power distribution to the wheels was by two different equations, depending on circumstances: 20% front and 80% rear or 35% front and 65% rear. The Delta S4's engine was completely new, rather than a much modified existing unit, a first for the Fiat Group. It was a refined four cylinder 'over-square' (bore 88.50 mm, stroke 71.50 mm) with an aluminium crankcase and a sump guard in light alloy. The aluminium cylinder sleeves were integrated into the crankcase and their surfaces hardened and made

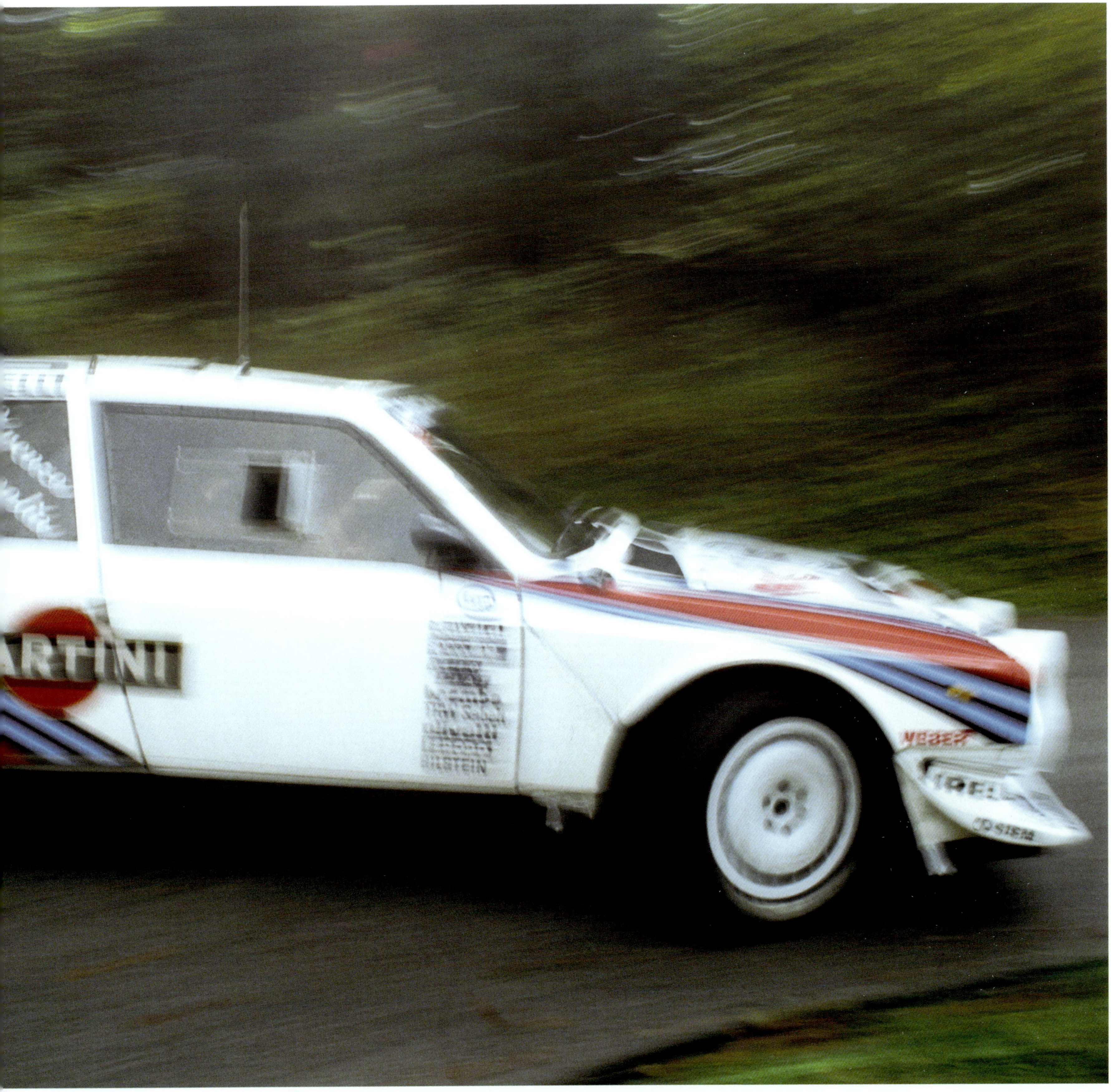
ARTINI
WEBER
BILSTEIN

LANCIA MARTINI
MARTINI
MAGNETI MARELLI
MARTINI
MAGNETI MARELLI
PIRELLI
WEBER
SIEM
Savara
speedline
FIAT
brembo
TRW Sabelt
olivetti
FERODO
BILSTEIN

more robust by a sophisticated new technology using ceramics. With a head of four valves per cylinder and twin overhead camshafts, supercharging with double air-to-air intercoolers and KKK gas turbine plus volumex (a system of volumetric compression patented by Lancia), this technological masterpiece reached a peak performance of around 480 hp at 5000 rpm: and all this without reliability problems. Such power meant 360 hp/litre and maximum torque of a remarkable 50kg/m at 5000 rpm: bear in mind the engine was only 1759 cc and the first question that has to be asked is how could all that power come from an engine which was so reliable. A tremendous achievement by the technical staff of Claudio Lombardi. Unfortunately, however, such commitment of men and technology led, as we know, to a tragic conclusion with the horrific Toivonen/Cresto accident during the Tour de Corse. And the car graced a farce of a world championship which was originally

Protruding lights profile the bold outline of the Delta S4, a supercar of extreme power and performance.

The rear light is identical to those of the LC 2 and Montecarlo Group 5: it takes its place in the tail of such high performance with sobriety.

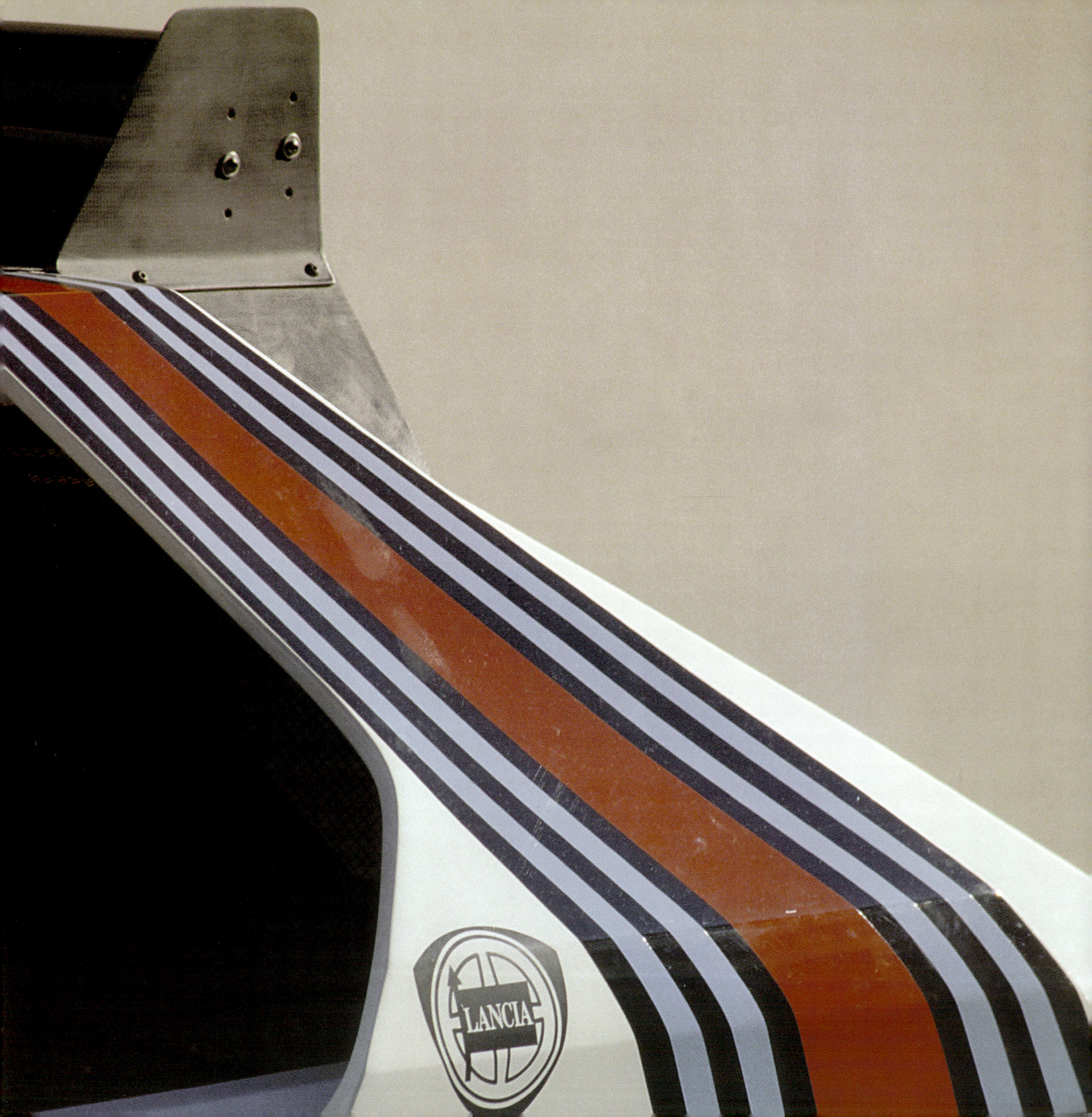
LANCIA

won by Markku Alen/Illka Kivimaki in the S4 but which was taken away from them after just over a week following unclear organisational disagreements. In effect, the Group B cars were "monsters" which almost refused to be tamed and driven on roads that were too narrow and dangerous for their space-age power. Regardless, Lancia did its best under Group B regulations until new world rally championship rules abolished such daunting concentrations of performance and technology in favour of mass produced Group A cars, which were certainly more controllable and brought with them a return to technology used in the production of cars for ordinary motorists. But climbing aboard an S4 once again during the preparation of this book had its effect on me, not least because I was to be driven by one of the world's greatest pilots who had achieved some of his greatest successes with the S4, double world champion Miki Biasion. He kindly accepted an invitation to slip behind the S4's wheel again, even if in such an extremely demanding cockpit. The predominant feeling for the passenger is one of being at the heart of a brutal force which shakes and accelerates all his cells in a most incredible way. In 2.7 seconds, we rocketed from 0-62 mph (0-100 km/h): a Formula One car could not do much better. This mind-blowing cocktail of power and relatively short gear ratios makes the speed of an S4 under acceleration comparable to that of an F16 fighter. To be aboard this "beast" provokes terrible emotion: immersed in an environ-

Left: Colours that flow and fly, the well-known stripes compliment perfectly the stylistic details of the S4.

In the dramatic nose made of a composite of different materials, the hidden headlamps seem to be afraid of the Group B Lancia's performance.

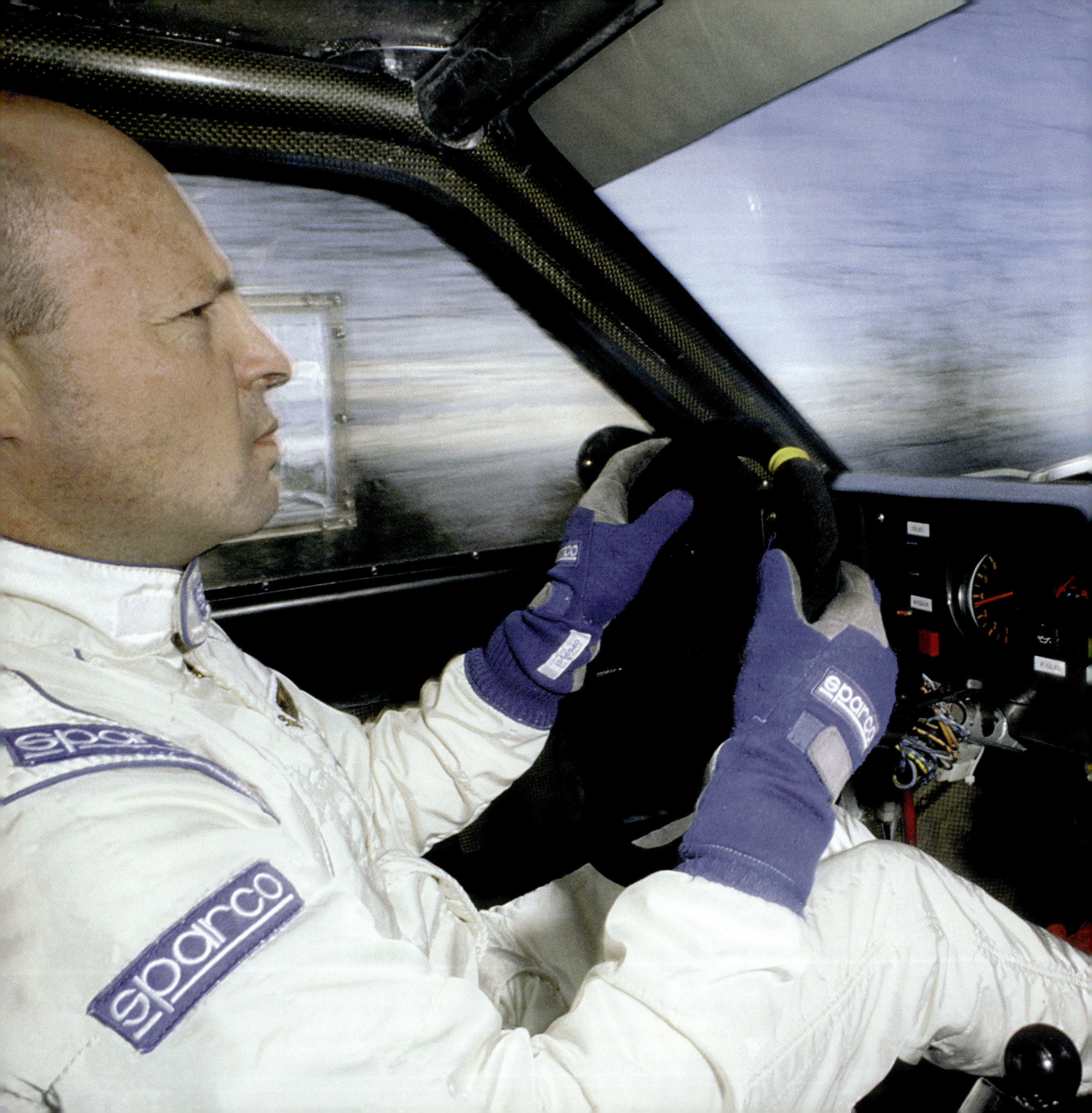
sparco
sparco
sparco

The most important dial: the means by which the power of the S4 is communicated to the driver.

Emotions a go-go: it is like being aboard a fighter aircraft on take-off.

ment pervaded by incredible sounds and vibrations, the mind moves with the speed with which the car is projected forward and my concentration was similar to that of the driver: I was only a little afraid, certainly less so than I expected. First, second, third and then we were travelling at the speed of sound! The S4 is a missile and that is probably the reason why Group B cars were retired so prematurely from the world championship: they became too dangerous because of their stratospheric performance. But we were just trying out the "monster" so as to bring back the unrepeatable sensations felt by the drivers when dominating around 500 horse power on roads normally used by ordinary mortals. There was no time to think; a driver must just work the pedals, manoeuvre levers and steer as fast as possible, because the next corner is already there and the road races past too fast by far; he must watch it with the eyes of a hawk. What a stressful way to drive a car: there again, are we sure we are talking about a car? Climbing to the peak of the mountain on this road, which was temporarily closed to traffic, Miki's expression changed completely. As he drove the S4 to the start line of "our" special stage, he was relaxed and chatty; then he seemed to transform himself into an astronaut a few seconds before his Shuttle is about to blast off. There was a special kind of light in his eyes and he kept his lips pursed, almost as if biting something. I tried to shoot some exciting pictures of the inside of the car, but the brutal acceleration of the S4 made the job almost impossible. Being in the car was such an emotional experience that it reminded me of how I felt when I was aboard one of the Frecce Tricolori Italian Air Force aerobatics team

The S4's four headlights are accompanied by four additional lamps.

The rear view mirror is anchored to a bar to limit vibration.

A typical full wheel of the S4 underlines the car's grit. On the bonnet was fitted a small refined wing in Kevlar, which improved the dissipation of hot air from the radiator. The three-quarter rear view emphasises the powerful body of this car, with its 480 hp.

planes during one of their displays: not at all bad. Miki drove fast, without problem: I felt that the car was completely under his control, which cannot be easy, to be sure, with 500 hp beneath his right foot. When the turbo came in and took over from the volumex, my back was pressed violently against the seat and my neck was unable to withstand the powerful "G" force the engine generated: by closing my eyes, I had the impression of being fired from a huge catapult. With every corner the "G" force seemed to increase, as did the speed of entry and mileage; every now and then the rear wheels tried to break away, but they were put back in their place again by precise steering input. Soon, Miki was driving as he did when he raced the S4 over some of the toughest terrain in the world rally championship and it was then that I understood why these Group B "monsters" were taken out of competition: they were literally missiles in flight and raced along roads lined by crowds of spectators: too dangerous! Miki also agreed and, at the top of the mountain which we conquered at stratospheric speed, he said it took a lot of guts to compete with a car of such power and performance when he was 30 years-old: he confessed he would not do so again now, because it is too stressful and risky. The Delta S4 is joy and pain all in one: it was a

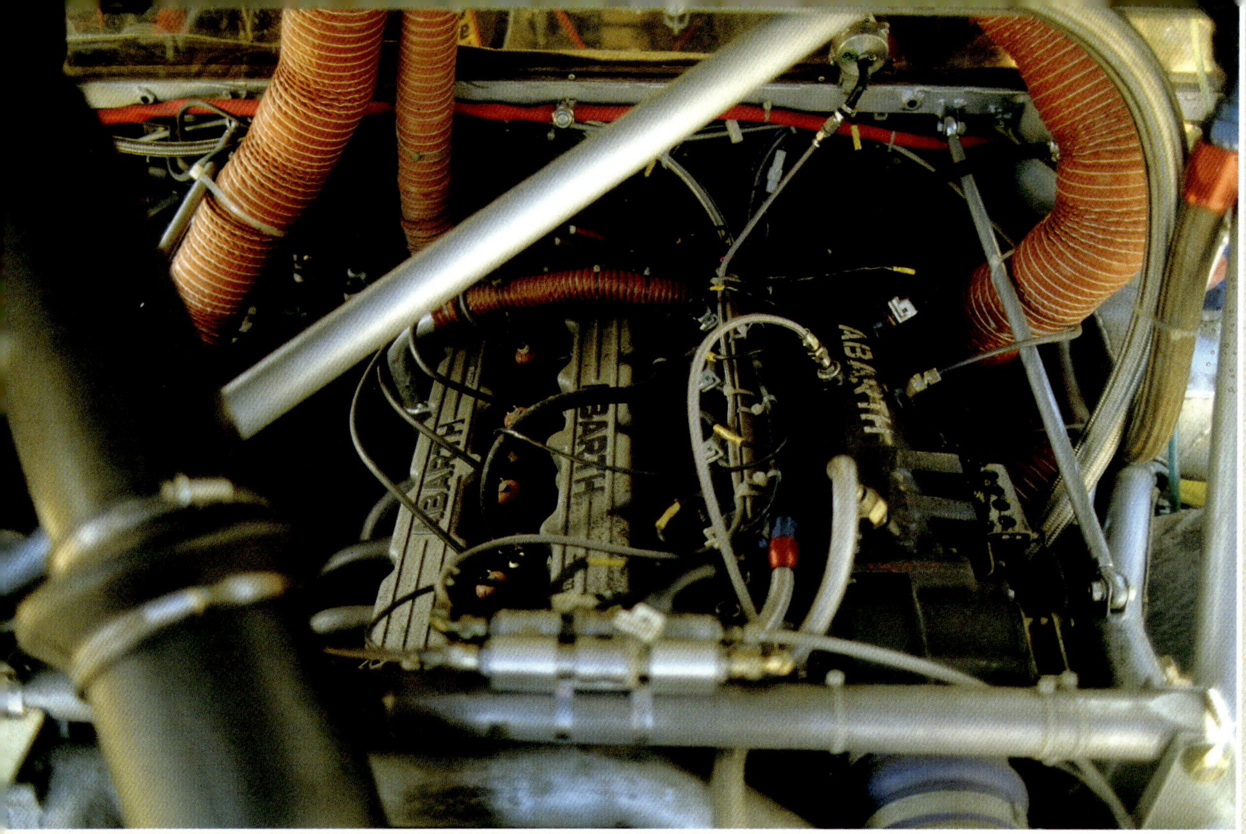
ABARTH

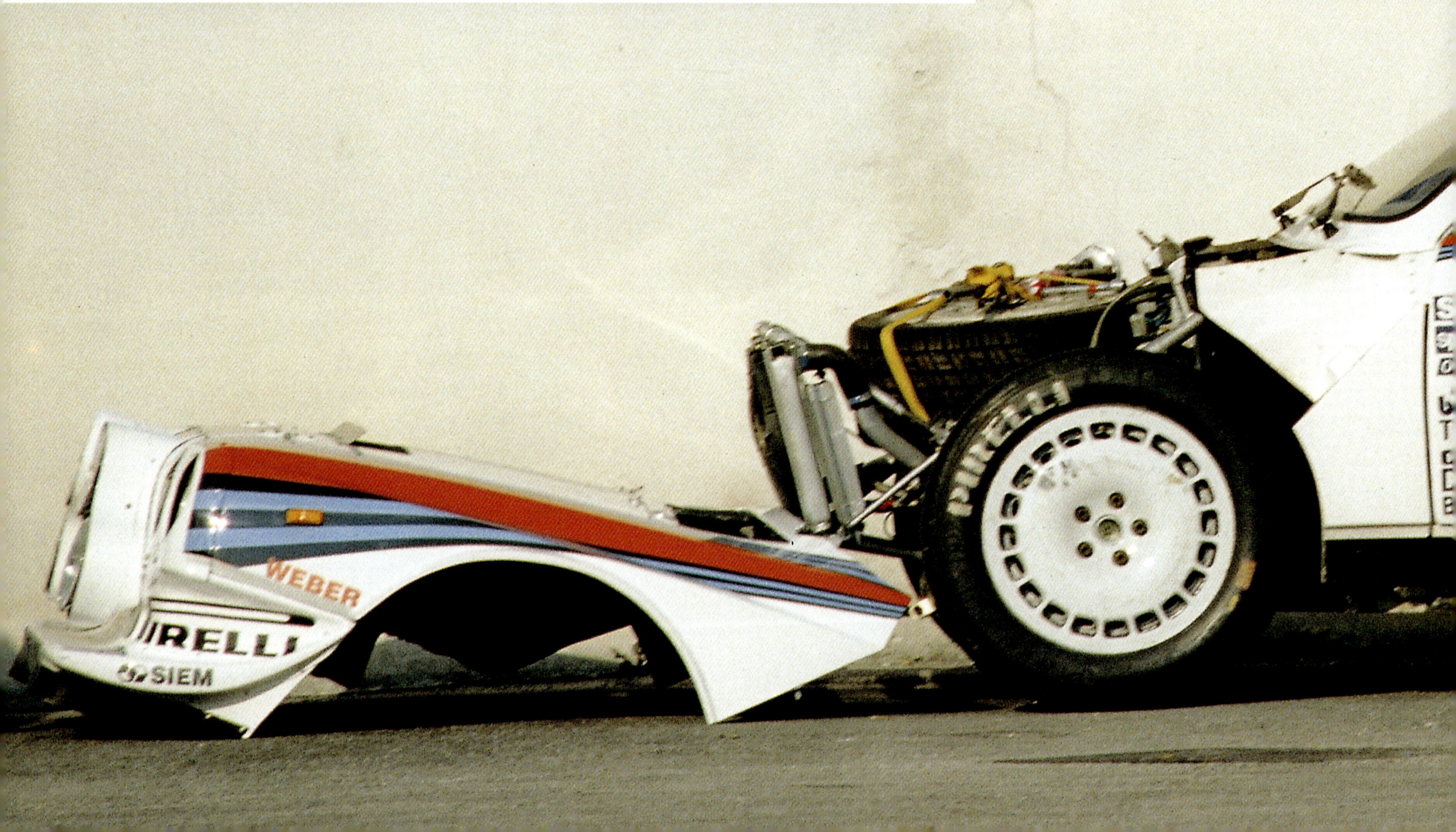
WEBER
IRELLI
SIEM
PIRELLI

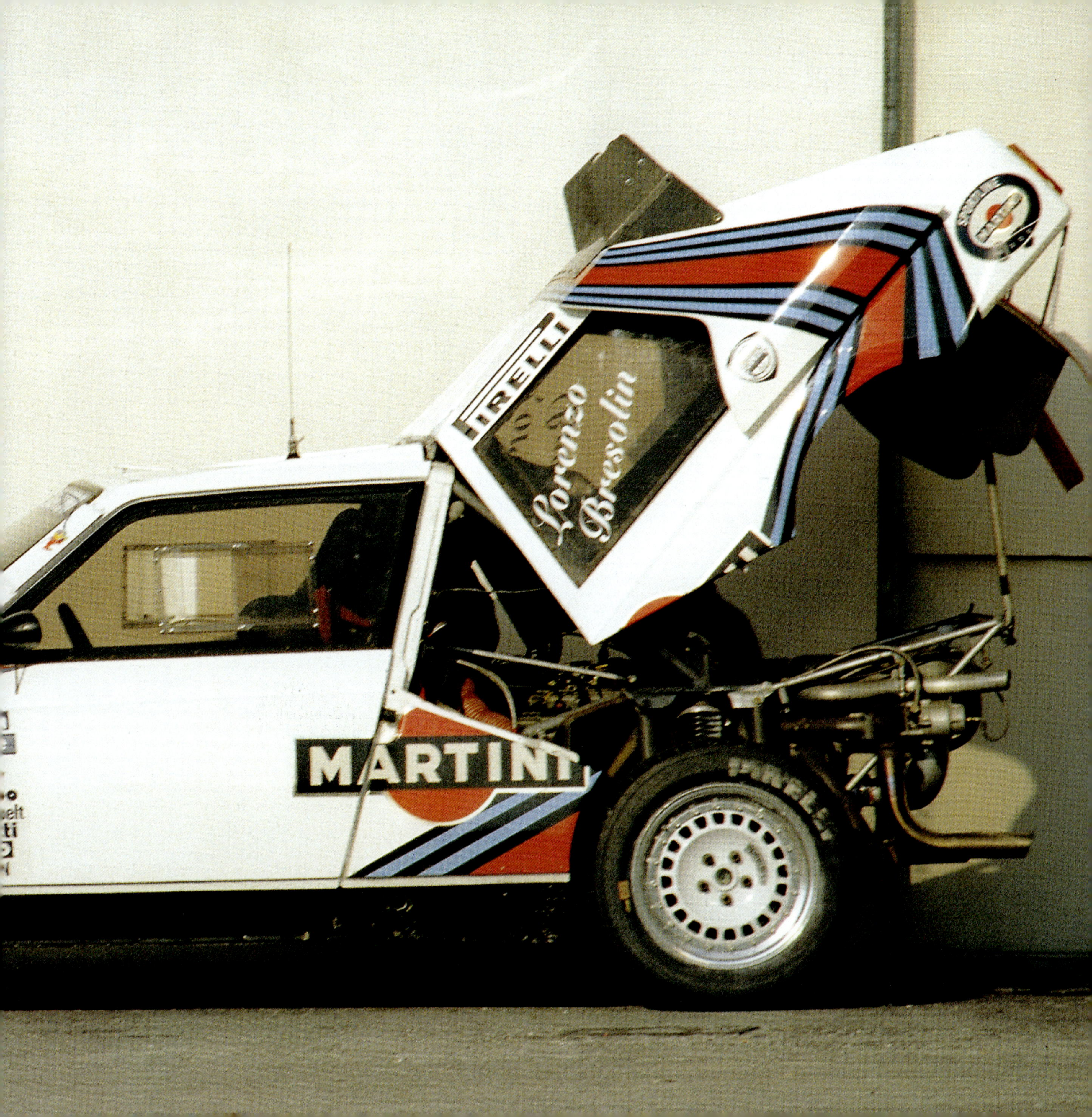
Lorenzo
Bresolin
MARTINI
PIRELLI

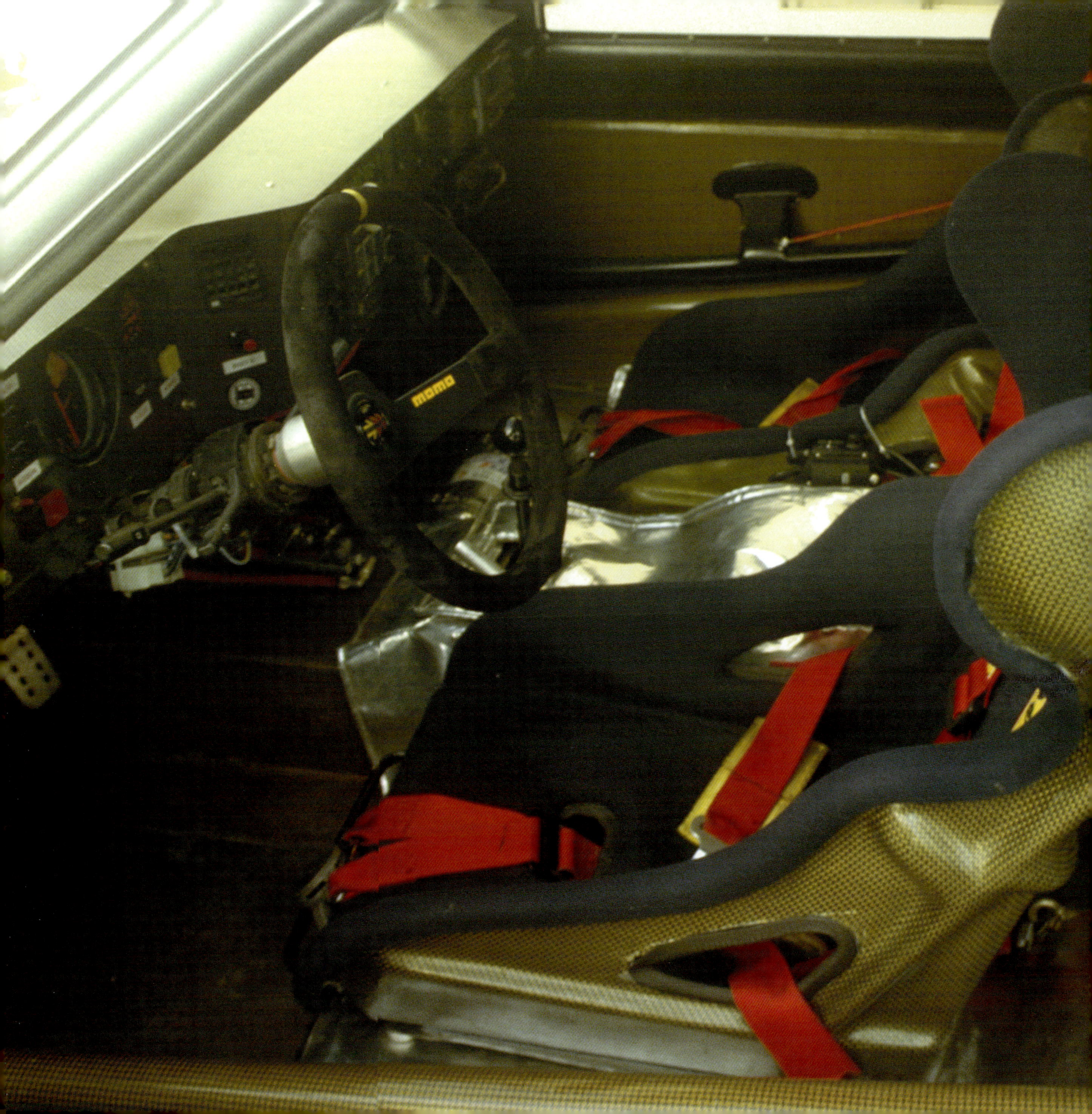
momo

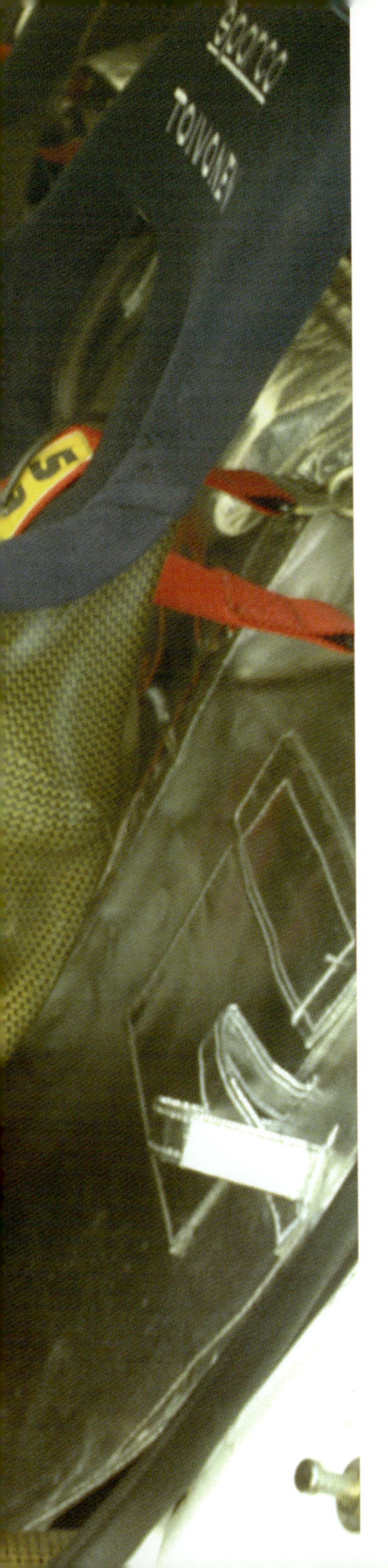

In the previous double page spread, the S4 shows its technological sole, a chassis of highly advanced conception, covered with a light skin of Kevlar: the whole thing comes to life thanks to an extremely powerful turbocharged engine with volumetric supercharger that generates a massive 480 hp. Inside, the car looks like a supersonic fighter: outside, even its rear end looks fearsome.

means of joining the fantastic world of a works team like Lancia, the dream of all drivers, but, at the same time, Biasion also recalls Toivonen's accident. "Harry was the one who best interpreted the characteristics of the S4, but it was probably his confidence, the continuing challenge of being on the limit with this 'monster', which led him to his death. I was the first to arrive at the scene of the accident, helpless in front of the blaze which, in practice, dictated the end of this car: a car which could be beyond the limit of human endeavour, if driven competitively for a long time". The S4 undoubtedly remains the maximum expression of the controversial category of Group B rally cars, and could certainly have been further developed to produce even higher performance and more power. But, without doubt, Lancia should be thanked for having the courage to retire their winner primarily for driver safety reasons.

Technical specification of the DELTA S4

ENGINE: four cylinders in line
ENGINE POSITION: rear, central, longitudinal
CUBIC CAPACITY: 1759 cc
BORE AND STROKE: 88.50x71.50 mm
DISTRIBUTION: two belt-driven overhead camshafts
NUMBER OF VALVES: 4 per cylinder
COMPRESSION RATIO: 7.5:1
FUEL SYSTEM: IAW Marelli-Weber integrated electronic injection and KKK turbo with double air-air intercooler, plus volumetric compressor
IGNITION: indirect electronic Weber-Marelli IAW
COOLING: forced circulation liquid
MAXIMUM POWER: 480 hp at 8400 rpm
MAXIMUM TORQUE: 50 kg/m at 5000 rpm
BODY: two-seater coupé, in Kevlar
CHASSIS: steel tube
SUSPENSION: independent front and rear, transversal arms, stabiliser bars, helicoidal springs, double rear hydraulic shock absorbers
TRANSMISSION: ZF five-speed gearbox with reverse, permanent four-wheel drive, Ferguson-type central viscose differential, self-blocking differential front and rear
CLUTCH: bi-disc, dry
BRAKES: self-ventilating discs front and rear
DIMENSIONS: length 4000 mm; width 1810 mm, height 1500 mm
WHEELBASE AND TRACK: 2440 mm-1500 mm front, 1520 mm rear
TYRES: front 235/660-16 front, 290/660-16 rear
WEIGHT, DRY: 900 kg
PERFORMANCE: maximum speed between 124 mph and 133 mph (200 km/h and 215 km/h), dependent on ratios
ACCELERATION: 0-62 mph (0-100 km/h) in 2.7 seconds (short ratios)

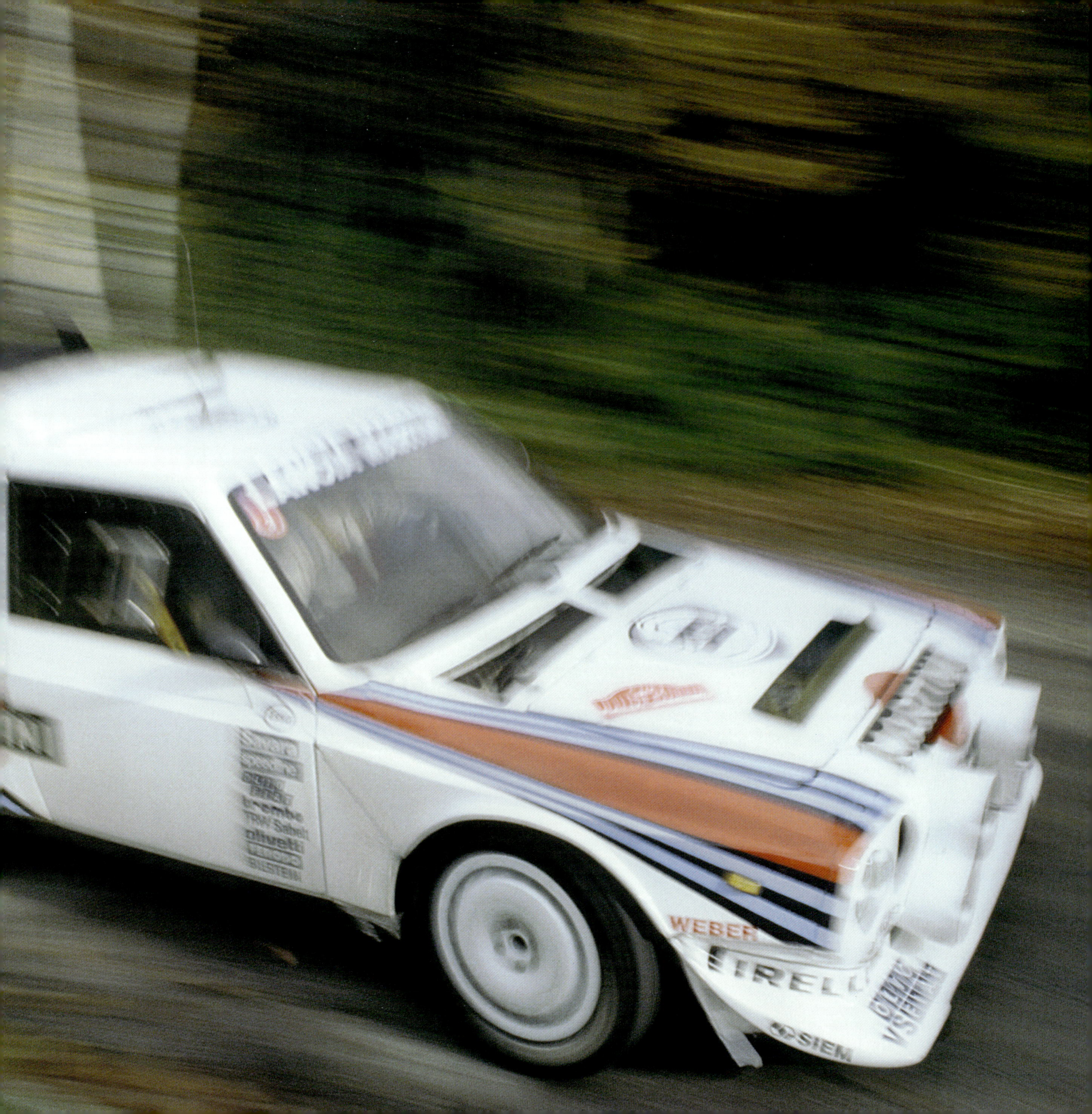
WEBER

Toivonen-Wilson enjoying themselves as they lift their S4's wheel in the mud of the 1985 RAC Rally of Great Britain; the two won the event, followed by Alen-Kivimaki's S4 in second place.

The photographs in these two pages appear by courtesy of Martini & Rossi.

The Biasion-Siviero S4 dropping down through the gears, with its exhaust spitting out a spectacular tongue of flame during the 1986 Rally of New Zealand.

Alen-Kivimaki in their S4 during the 1986 Monte Carlo Rally.

Toivonen-Cresto and their S4 in action during their last tragic in Tour de Corse in 1986.

DELTA 4WD

Stepping out of the S4, climbing aboard the HF 4WD and driving the new Group A car was difficult to begin with: the S4's thrillingly violent sensation of power was not there, but the need for greater safety meant drivers had to get used to new and more "human" limits. Even Miki Biasion, who won two world drivers' championships and contributed to two world manufacturers' titles, confirmed that, in the first rally of 1987, the 4WD seemed too slow. In reality, though, that was just an impression because later the evolution of the Group A led to performance similar to that of the "terrible" Group B cars, even if completely safe and manageable as well as less taxing on the driver and navigator. After the drastic changes imposed by Fédération Internationale de L'Automobile following the horrific fatal accidents, particularly the loss of Toivonen and Cresto during the Tour de Corse, and the general confusion of the 1986 rally season, Group B were outlawed; the cars' exceptional performance was regarded by many, including the drivers, as too difficult and demanding to be controlled safely. Yet it was in that climate of extreme uncertainty that Lancia quickly came up with an idea that made it the king of world championship rallying for several years. The new Group A regulations dictated that each car's power had to be kept in check by flanging the turbo so that the amount of available power was notably reduced; so the rules would not allow a sufficient increase in engine power to ensure Lancia's superiority. The only area which could provide a marked improvement in performance was four-wheel drive: by further developing its recently acquired know-how in the field, the Turin manufacturer created a system of permanent four-wheel drive which performed well and was highly reliable. It was a system with three differentials: the usual front one, the central unit was an epicycloidal limited slip diff with a Ferguson-type viscose joint and a Torsen rear differential. The point of departure for this new world

LANCIA
MICHELIN
MICHELIN
4x4
Savara
OLIO
FIAT
ESSO
FERODO
BILSTEIN
MAGNETI
MARELLI

MICHELIN

ARTINI

championship adventure was, finally, a more human car, a four-door saloon in which Lancia wholeheartedly believed and which, commercially, represented a large share of the market. In its four-wheel drive form, the Delta was the ideal car with which to compete against other teams that were so experienced in all-wheel drive. The origin of this 4x4 Lancia can be found some years further back, at the 1982 Turin Motor Show, where a Delta prototype made its debut with 4x4 emblazoned down its flanks. This Delta, with an identical body to its two-wheel drive stablemates, was fitted with Beta coupé wheels, a big spoiler and was sprayed in a sober metallic grey: it certainly never alluded to its enormous potential of a few years down the road as the antagonist par excellence, feared and revered by all its opponents in world championship rallying. This experimental prototype had a 1585 cc engine with twin overhead camshafts, turbo, intercooler and a 130 hp power output: a power unit able to propel the first four-wheel drive Delta at 118 mph (190 km/h). But the car

Thanks to the multi-coloured livery, the sides of the HF 4WD seem almost like those of a coupé.

The first of the Delta generation were the narrowest and "kindest" of the line.

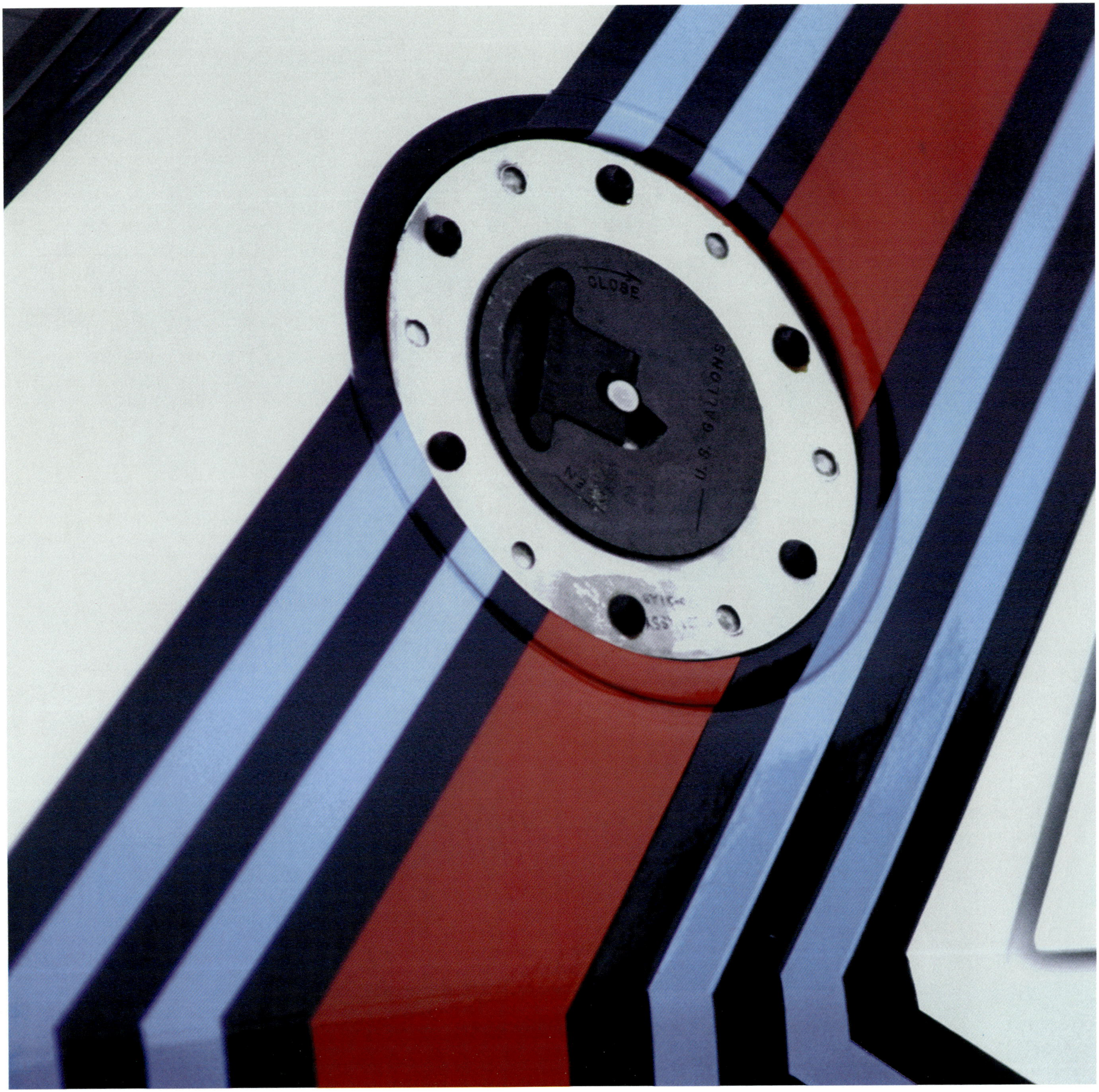
CLOSE
U.S. GALLONS

The wheels, with their 19 "spokes" radiating from the hub rather like the sun's rays, gave the Delta 4WD a look of gritty determination which, derived from the road-going Lancia, had notable sporting charm.

Opposite page: The sports-type petrol tank cap with its shiny surround stood out well from the car's multi-coloured flanks.

that gave birth to the 4WD had little in common with its sibling. The new rally car's engine became a 1995 cc turbo unit with overboost and generated 165 hp at 5250 rpm. Large logos appeared along its sides and more refined badges of identification were placed on the radiator grill and tail. Soon to become the dominator of the 1988 season, this car was developed in the Lancia racing department under the direction of engineer Claudio Lombardi and, among other things, was the subject of careful bodybuilding. The monocoque was reinforced with a steel tube structure (rollbar inside the cockpit), the shock absorbers were strengthened to stand the considerable stress of ral-

The Speedline wheels first fitted to the Delta 4WD later became the preferred units.

The white body's "decoration" started with class from the rear light.

The cylinder head was painted red to underline its sporting temperament.

Headlights and radiator grill were identical to those of the road car. Only the bumper bar tow ring was added.

The "little geese", as they were christened, improved internal ventilation.

lying and a dome bar was fitted to the shock absorber supports in the engine compartment to reinforce the car's front end. The engine was modified as far as the rules allowed to gain a few more horse power, despite the rule governing turbo flanging: that is how the 4WD's power was increased to 265 hp at 6250 rpm, considerably more than the road car's output. But torque was the most impressive element on this car: 39 kg/m at just 3000 rpm. So it is easy to see why the Delta 4WD, with such a high degree of torque and four-wheel drive, had an unchallenged liquidity of action and, therefore, driveability at all revs: an incredible advantage in rallying, in which sharp corners alternate with fast straights. The progression of this little saloon was certainly one of its winning traits. With a weight of 1130 kg and a length of 3.89 metres, the Delta 4WD was one of the best conceived, most agile rally cars of the period: its Garrett T3 turbo (the same further developed unit would be fitted to all Deltas until the end of

Trip master, fuses, rollbar, additional instruments on the dash distinguish this Delta and add to its appeal. The livery was by the specialist company Nitro C, which created all the Lancia Martinis' paint schemes.

This car seemed at its meanest when seen in action.

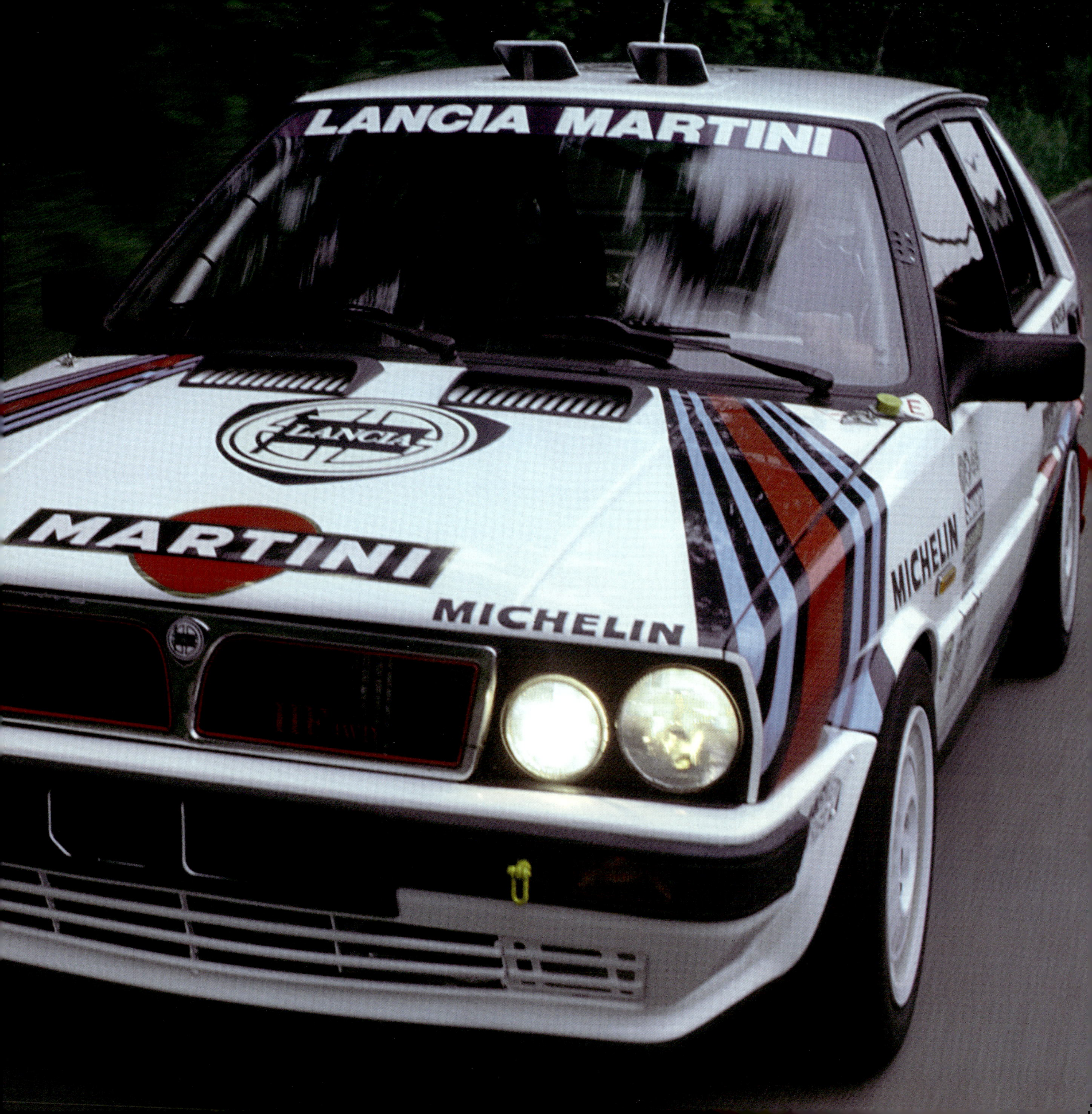
LANCIA MARTINI
LANCIA
MARTINI
MICHELIN
MICHELIN

The air intakes and the 4WD HF badge on the front end of the car both help distinguish a four-wheel drive Lancia.

the model's motor sport career) enabled its drivers to even exploit its power at low revs, always maintaining traction at an optimum level. It was due to all of these technological advantages and an exceptional team of drivers, among them Juha Kankkunen, Miki Biasion and Didier Auriol, that, in the first season under FISA's new Group A regulations, Lancia and the Delta 4WD won seven world championship rallies out of 13, dominating the manufacturers' championship and laying a foundation for many more years of superiority. In fact, Miki Biasion was able to win the 1988 world drivers' championship having showed right from the start which car was going to dictate the pace for several seasons to come. The opposition had been warned!

Opposite page: The characteristic orange plastic wing-type mudguard behind the wheel is a trademark of almost all Lancia rally cars.

87

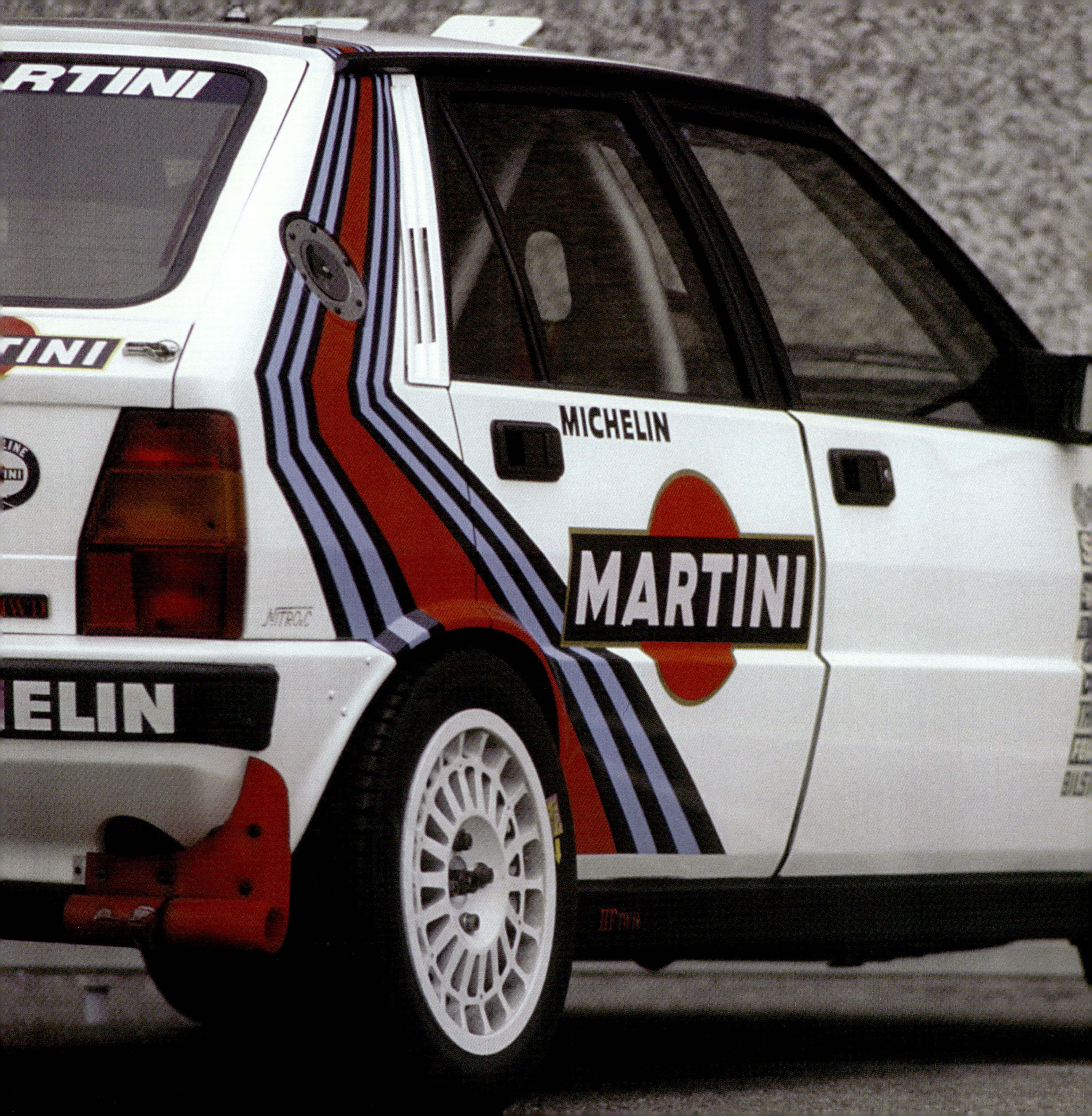

MARTINI
MICHELIN
MARTINI

Technical specification of the DELTA 4WD

ENGINE: four cylinders in line
ENGINE POSITION: front, transverse
CUBIC CAPACITY: 1995 cc
BORE AND STROKE: 84x90 mm
DISTRIBUTION: twin belt-driven overhead camshafts
NUMBER OF VALVES: two per cylinder
COMPRESSION RATIO: 6.5:1
FUEL SYSTEM: Weber-Marelli IAW electronic injection, Garrett T3 turbo, overboost
IGNITION: electronic, Weber-Marelli IAW
COOLING: liquid, front radiator
MAXIMUM POWER: 265 hp at 6750 rpm
MAXIMUM TORQUE: 39 kg/m at 3000 rpm
BODY: four-door saloon in steel
CHASSIS: load-bearing bodyshell plus frame in special steel
SUSPENSION: independent all-round, front stabiliser bar, double rear shock absorbers
TRANSMISSION: five-speed and reverse ZF gearbox with front linkage; permanent four-wheel drive with three differentials (central epicycloidal with Ferguson limited slip joint)
CLUTCH: bi-disc, dry
BRAKES: perforated, self-ventilating disc brakes front and rear
DIMENSIONS: length 3890 mm, width 1620 mm, height 1360 mm
WHEELBASE AND TRACK: 2480 mm – 1430 mm front, 1440 mm rear
TYRES: 210/595-15 front and rear with 8x15J wheels
DRY WEIGHT: 1130 kg
PERFORMANCE: maximum speed about 124 mph (200 km/h), depending on gear ratios
ACCELERATION: 0-62 mph (0-100 km/h) in less than five seconds

MARTINI & ROSSI
MARTINI & ROSSI
PIRELLI
PIRELLI
SIEM
SIEM
LANCIA MARTINI
MARTINI

Left, large photograph: Alen-Kivimaki in a controlled slide on an unmade special stage during the 1987 Olympus Rally. Small photograph: Kankkunen-Piironen on snow in the 1987 Rally of Monte Carlo.

Alen-Kivimaki on asphalt, watched by a large crowd during the 1987 Rally of Portugal.

Alen-Kivimaki with Delta 4WD number 1 during the 1987 San Remo Rally.

Biasion-Siviero on the rough in the 1987 San Remo.

The photographs on pages 90 and 91 appear by courtesy of Martini & Rossi.

LANCIA
MARTINI
MICHELIN
MICHEL
TURBO GARRETT
TO 86305M
CARELLO
GARRETT TUR
CARELL

DELTA INTEGRALE 16V

A winning exploit in colour: the 1989 Rally of San Remo was dominated by the new Lancia Delta Integrale 16V, which appeared in a vivacious and unusual racing red livery, decorated with Martini stripes of a different format. This derivative, which brought the new four valves per cylinder head to rallying which was first fitted to the road car, had wider wings like those of the 1988 HF Integrale and a more roguish looking additional power bump on the bonnet to make room for the new, uprated engine and its bigger head. The Delta Integrale 16V was an evolution of the HF 4WD, embodying a considerable number of modifications. An intermediate HF Integrale, in fact, with bigger tyres and new air intakes on the bonnet; the Integrale was mechanically closer to the first Delta rally car and, compared to the original, only slightly modified mechanically. The red Delta HF Integrale made the briefest of appearances in the world championship: immediately after the San Remo it had gone back to its original white and sponsor's coloured stripes. But the red car remains a rarity in Lancia Martini history, not least because it won a world championship rally on its first and only appearance. The mechanics of the car were based on the successful four-cylinder 1995 cc engine, fitted with a 16 valve cylinder head that produced 30 hp more than the previous model, developing 295 hp at 7000 rpm.

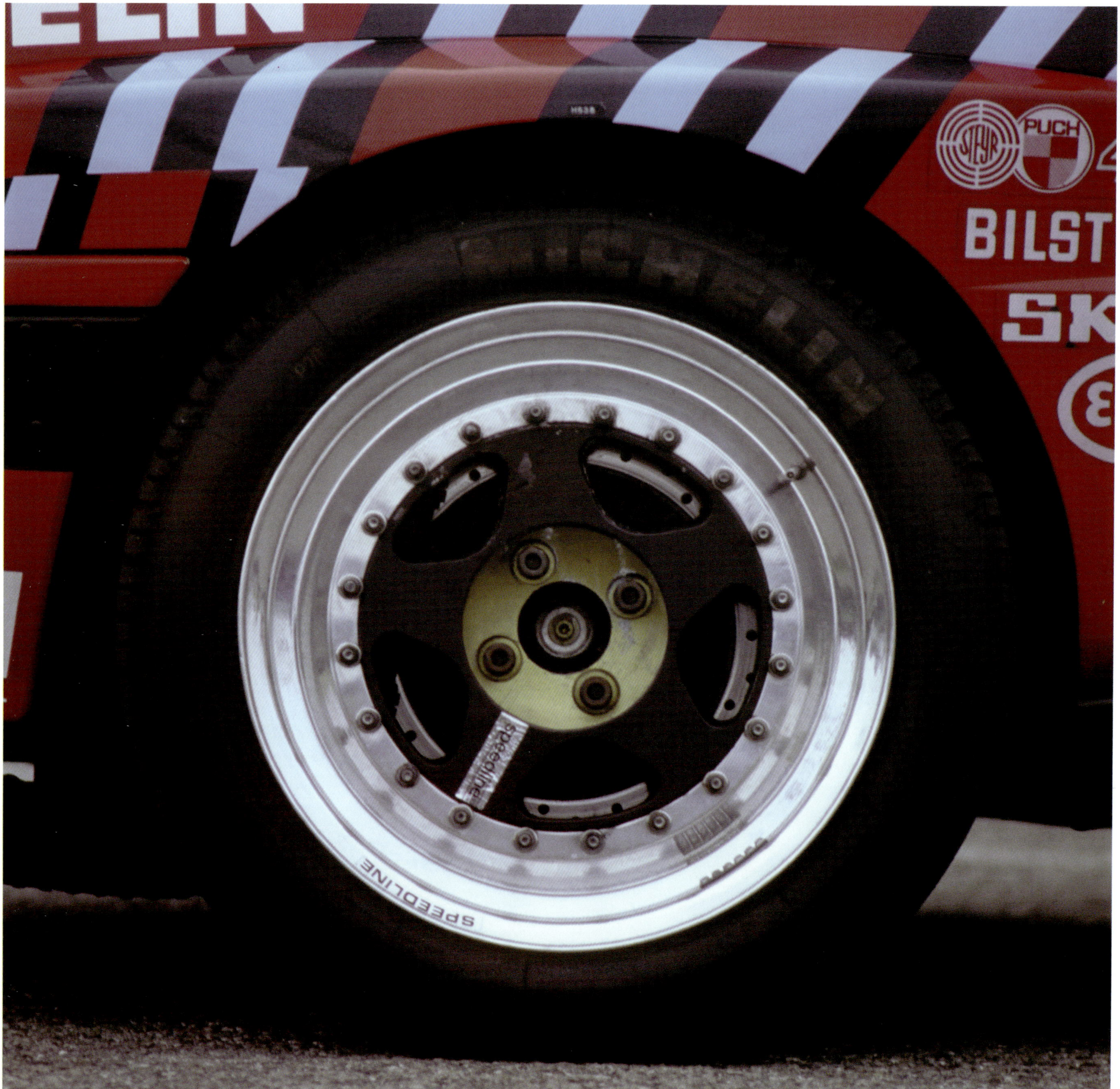
PUCH
BILST
speedline
SPEEDLINE

Compared to the HF 4WD, the most powerful muscles of the Integrale 16V were more than evident: the bulging wings and bonnet accentuated its potent image.

The curve of the wing flowed into the centre of the headlamps. The white lettering of the sponsors' logos stood out against the red background.

The new sectional wheels, with their rims in bright aluminium, showed the self-ventilating disc brakes.

MARTINI
SPORTLINE
MARTINI

MICHELIN
4x4
BILSTEIN
SKF
Esso
pharmagel
speedline
Fiat
Lubrificanti
brembo
TRW Sabelt
FERODO
MAGNETI MARELLI
WEBER
SELÈNIA
MOTOR OIL
Valeo

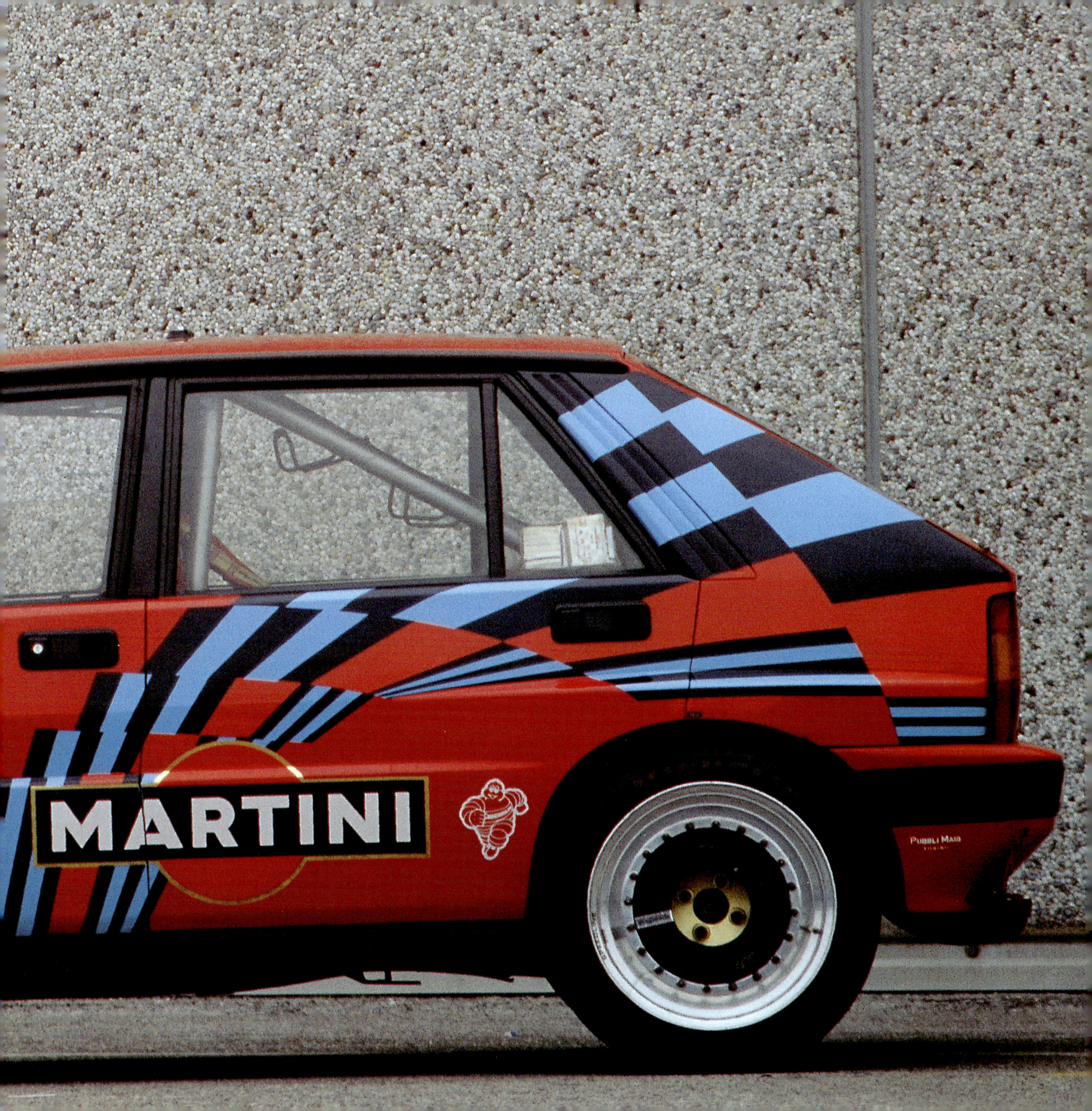
MARTINI

In the previous double page spread, the Integrale 16V and its periscope-type air intakes on the roof. The red livery was used for just one rally.

The Kevlar seats were certainly not suited to people of robust build, but fitted the drivers perfectly. The small steering wheel was meant for speedy communication with the asphalt.

The layout of the sponsor's coloured stripes changed the appearance of the car radically.

The 16V's engine had a turbo with smaller runners to improve sharpness of response and generated a maximum torque of 41 kg/m at 4500 rpm. But the new developments built into this Lancia Martini in red were not just limited to fitting a 16V cylinder head: they also included the engine's compression ratio which, compared to the 4WD, was reduced to 6.5:1, new, wider Speedline sectional alloy wheels, more powerful brakes and new identification badges on the radiator grill and hatchback. The rally car's six-speed gearbox was made more robust, as was the road version's five-speed box. Lancia entered two red-liveried Deltas for the 1989 Rally of San Remo, one for Biasion and the other for Didier Auriol. The Frenchman had an accident during the rally and destroyed his car but Biasion went on to win. The surviving car, photographed for this book, was later passed on to the Jolly Club team, which had been competing with Lancias for some time. Dario Cerrato drove the privately entered Integrale 16V in a number of rallies and also used it to test Lancia's electronic clutch, which was destined for motor sport. This car was returned to its original victorious red after it was bought by a collector, who much admired the Integrale 16V success period. In 1989, when Miki Biasion won his second world drivers' championship and Lancia the manufacturers' title again, the Integrale 16V won seven of a possible 13 rallies. The importance of this particular evolution of Lancia's first four-wheel drive was fundamental to the future ambitions of the company in the world championship, in that the 16V was the longest lasting model in the history of the Delta; to reach the final, definitive evolution would take another three years and herald the retirement of Lancia from rallying, after winning five manufacturers' and four drivers' titles. The future "Deltona" or big Delta (as a broad cross-section of the Italian public baptised the last of Lancia's integrales) was no longer rallied by its manufacturer, but privately by the Jolly Club in the red, white and blue of its sponsor, Martini: in 1992, the car won its sixth and last world manufacturers' championship, having achieved a record nine victories out of a possible 10. A distinguished career had come to an end.

The new grills in the convex bonnet for better dissipation of heat, built up in the engine compartment.

The fragmented progression of the new Martini livery's stripes on the red background.

99

Technical specification of the DELTA INTEGRALE 16V

ENGINE: four cylinders in line
ENGINE POSITION: front, transverse
CUBIC CAPACITY: 1995 cc
BORE AND STROKE: 84x90 mm
DISTRIBUTION: twin belt-driven overhead camshafts
NUMBER OF VALVES: four per cylinder
COMPRESSION RATIO: 6.5:1
FUEL SYSTEM: Weber-Marelli IAW electronic injection, Garrett T3 turbo, overboost
IGNITION: electronic, Weber-Marelli IAW
COOLING: liquid, front radiator
MAXIMUM POWER: 295 hp at 7000 rpm
MAXIMUM TORQUE: 41 kg/m at 4500 rpm
BODY: four-door saloon, steel
CHASSIS: load-bearing bodyshell plus frame in special steel
SUSPENSION: independent all round, front stabiliser bar, double rear shock absorbers
TRANSMISSION: six-speed plus reverse ZF gearbox with front insertion, permanent four-wheel drive with three differentials (central epicycloidal with Ferguson limited slip joint
CLUTCH: bi-disc, dry
BRAKES: perforated self-ventilating discs all round
DIMENSIONS: length 3900 mm, width 1685 mm, height 1360 mm.
WHEELBASE AND TRACK: 2480 mm – 1512 mm front, 1466 mm rear
TYRES: 210-590/15 all round on x15J rims
WEIGHT, DRY: 1100 kg
PERFORMANCE: maximum speed 106 mph-124 mph (170 km/h-210 km/h), depending on ratios
ACCELERATION: 0-62 mph (0-100 km/h) in 4.2 seconds with short gear ratios

ABARTH
cl.
X 1000
10
9
8
7
6
5
4
3
2
TEMP.
OLIO
PRESS.
BENZINA
10
20
30
40
60
ELETE
TEMP.
ACQUA

The photographs on pages 102 and 103 appear by courtesy of Martini & Rossi.

Above: A spectacular picture of the Kankkunen-Piironen Delta Integrale 16V charging through a ford during the 1991 Rally of Argentina. Below, sunset on a rocky stage of the same rally.

Above: Kankkunen-Piironen in the Delta Integrale 16V during the 1989 Rally of Portugal.
Below: Biasion-Siviero on an asphalt special stage in the 1990 Rally of Monte Carlo.

DELTA SAFARI

Hunting big game ... not exotic wild animals, but victory! Perhaps the most fascinating rally of them all, Lancia won the African Safari rally with its four-wheel drive Delta in 1988, 1989 and 1991 and, as the results show, it was an ideal car with which to challenge the desert and its dangers. Participation in this most beautiful and spectacular event demands a major commitment in terms of personnel and investment to cover all the essentials and start the rally with a competitive car. Lancia, for instance, assigned about 100 employees to the task and never invested less than five months in preparing its quest for success in the Kenya marathon. Support vehicles were highly sophisticated and included three helicopters, which constantly shadowed the Deltas during testing and the rally itself and a fleet of trucks carrying spare parts and equipment to the service areas which were set up along the route. The cars that took part in this punishing rally had to have mechanical characteristics and bodies prepared especially for the event. So the appearance of the Deltas and their support vehicles corresponded in spectacular fashion to the environment in which the rally took place. Compared to their sister cars built to take part in other world championship rallies, the Safari Deltas looked like aliens from another planet: ground height was comparable to that of off-road vehicles, batteries of lights capable of illuminating a Hollywood set jutted out from every part of the front end and protection typical of armoured vehicles seen in the most far-fetched American action films shielded the bow. In fact, those special steel guards on the front of the cars, called "roo-bars" in rally slang, were gigantic tubular steel structures fitted to the cars by special

105

and extremely robust attachments to the chassis: their job was to protect the radiator grill, radiator and front lights from any kind of impact. And it is not difficult to imagine the effect of contact with debris spat out from under the wheels of opponents up front when racing along at Safari Rally speeds, which often reached 125 mph. In fact, the 1989 Safari Rally Lancia Delta Integrale 16Vs in these photographs were capable of 140 mph. They had very different gear ratios to those of their stable mates driven in all of the other world championship rallies: first was very short, used to get the car out of awkward predicaments and in emergencies, while sixth was set so that the car could accelerate to its 140 mph maximum. This in spite of being heavier (1270 kg) than the asphalt cars and the notable aerodynamic encumbrances of the Safari version. Special equipment with which to protect the underbody was also fundamental to this car, even if invisible except at the front: the Safari Delta was armed with a Kevlar shield running the length of its underbelly to protect the car's precious mechanics. But the large machete was an odd addition, inserted as it was, perhaps for luck, in special housing in the rear door. Mechanically, the Delta destined for the African desert underwent minor modifications which increased the engine's power output by about 30 hp, while at the same time ensuring everything linked to the car's reliability was minutely checked. In the same way, the Lancia rally team also prepared numerous car washes

Inside the car, a protective film was applied to the side windows to reduce cockpit heat.

Without doubt, the battery of lights on the nose of the Safari Delta gave it a spectacularly dramatic appearance.

VITALONI
MARTINI
SAFARI RALLY
MARTINI
7
KENYA
FINA
CECOMP
SELENIA
sparco
brembo
TRW Sabelt
CHAMPION
SKF
BILSTEIN
MICHELIN
WEBER

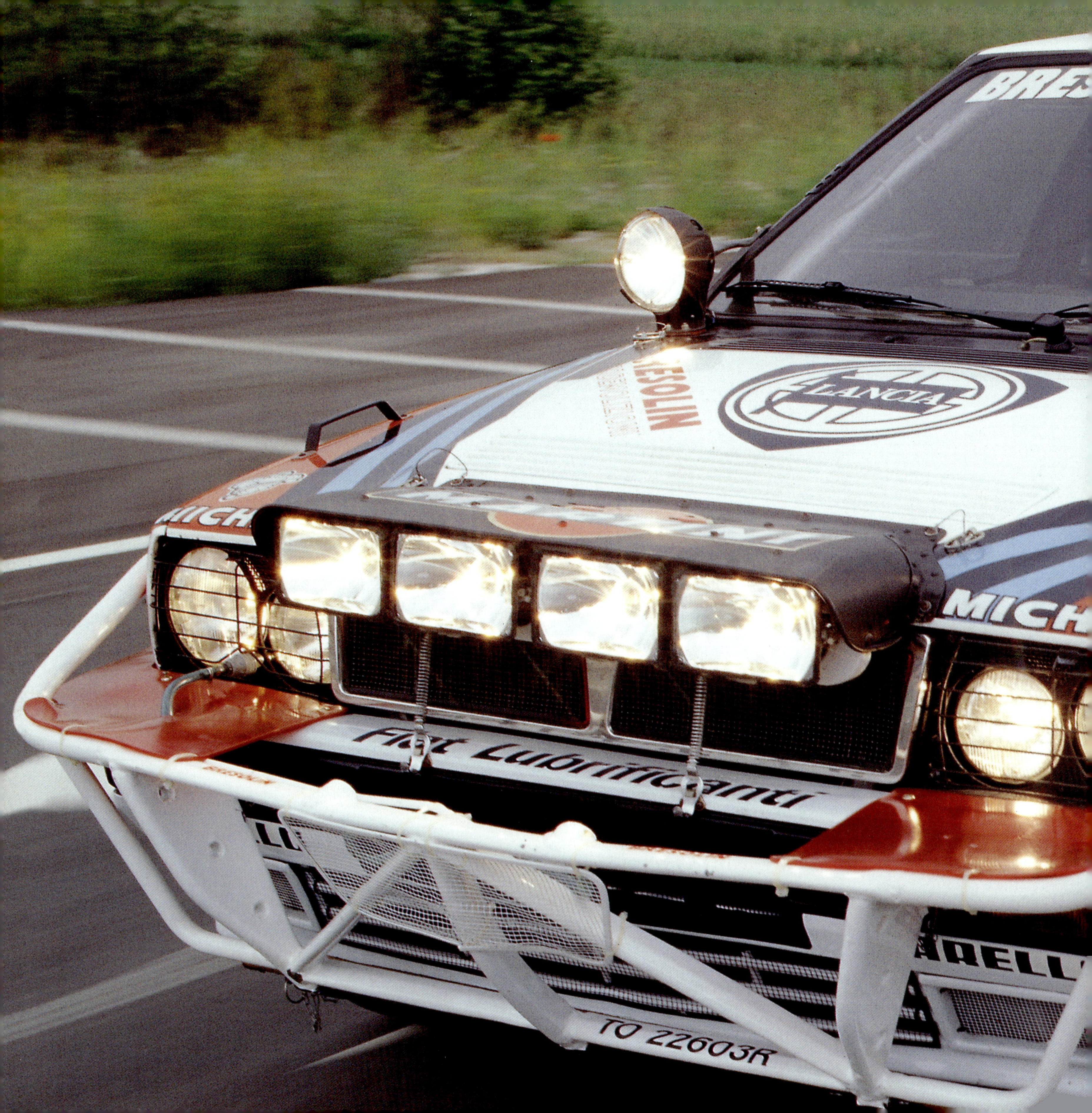
LANCIA
Fiat Lubrificanti
TO 22603R

AUTODEMOLIZIONI
VITALONI
SAFARI RALLY
MARTINI
MARTINI
M. BIASION
T. SIVIERO
FINA
CECOMP
SELENIA
sparco
KENYA
MICHELIN
MAGNETI MARELLI
WEBER
SELENIA
MOTOR OIL

A detailed picture of some of the Safari Delta's strengthening: the engine was given more horsepower with which to face the African desert.

Like the fronts, the rear bumper bars were steel reinforced, a hallmark of the Safari.

Modifications to the Delta for Safari duty were expensive: carbon fibre was used liberally.

The petrol tank was separate from the cockpit and had a silvered surface, embellished with the Lancia shield.

A stern warning: the word STACK repeated three times confirmed that over-revving was imminent.

110

The considerable height of the Safari Delta was evident at first glance.

along the rally route to allow the crews to stop and have their car radiators and other exposed components cleaned of mud and sand deposits. Designed to avoid internal flooding when speeding through deep water, one of the Safari Delta's many expensive modifications included a Kevlar superstructure which covered the roll-bar on the sides of the doors: it was sufficiently high to protect the crew from flooding in water more than 70 cm deep. Occasionally, exhaust pipes were also lengthened and fitted with a periscope-type underwater snorkel so that they remained substantially above the high-water mark. On the rev counter near the red zone was the word STACK in capital letters. It was really the name of the instrument's manufacturer but for the Italians it had a kind of emergency sound to it so STACK also became a word of admonition. If the rev counter needle got close to it that meant the moment had arrived for the driver to lift off the accelerator - immediately! The crews which took part in the Safari Rally had available to them almost NASA-type space technology with which to compete safely in the desert. On the other hand, the fascination of the African continent and the image boost Lancia achieved by winning this event justified the sacrifices and cost it demanded.

Technical specification of the SAFARI DELTA 16V

ENGINE: four cylinders in line
ENGINE POSITION: front, transverse
CUBIC CAPACITY: 1995 cc
BORE AND STROKE: 84 x 90 mm
DISRIBUTION: twin belt-driven overhead camshafts
NUMBER OF VALVES: four per cylinder
COMPRESSION RATIO: 6.5:1
FUEL SYSTEM: Weber-Marelli I.A.W. electronic injection, Garrett T3 turbocharger, overboost.
IGNITION: Weber-Marelli IAW electronic
COOLING: liquid, front radiator
MAXIMUM POWER: 330 hp at 7500 rpm
MAXIMUM TORQUE: 43 kgm at 4700 rpm
BODY: four seater saloon, steel body
CHASSIS: load-bearing monocoque with frame in special steel
SUSPENSION: independent all round, front stabiliser bar, double rear shock absorbers.
TRANSMISSION: six–speed and reverse ZF gearbox with front engagement, permanent four-wheel drive with three differentials (central epicycloidal, with limited slip Ferguson joint)
CLUTCH: dry bi-disc
BRAKES: perforated, self-ventilating discs front and rear
DIMENSIONS: length – 4100 mm with roo-bar, width – 1685 mm, height – 1470 mm
WHEELBASE AND TRACK: 2480 mm – 1512 mm front, 1466 mm rear
TYRES: 6 1/2 x 15 rims front and rear
DRY WEIGHT: 1270 kg
PERFORMANCE: maximum speed 140 mph

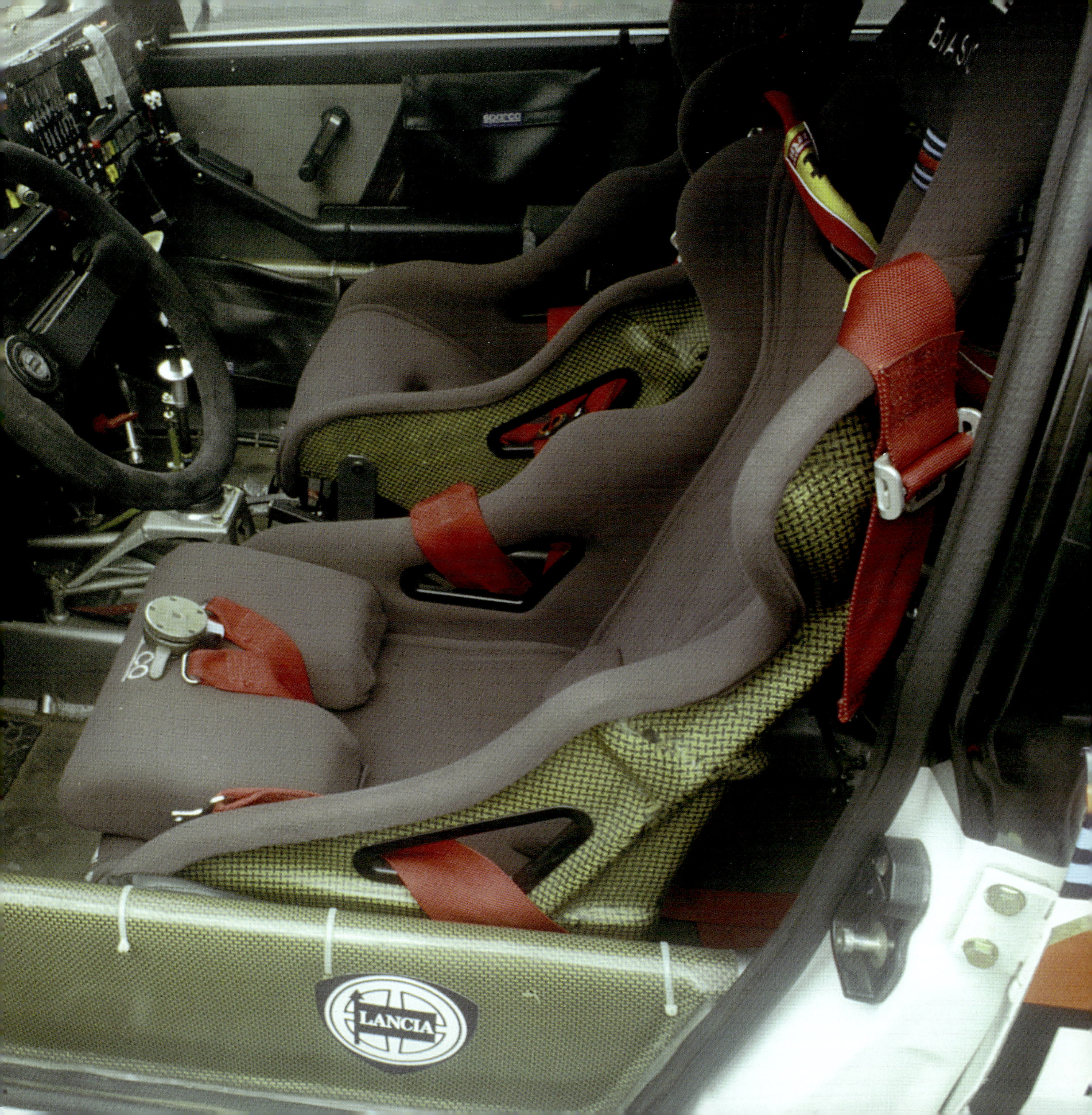
LANCIA

The photographs on pages 114 and 115 are published by courtesy of Martini & Rossi.

A spectacular charge at speed through a ford during the 1991 Safari Rally, won by Juha Kankkunen in this 'armoured' Delta 16V, which looks more like a speedboat cutting through the water than a car competing in a rally.

The Safari environment is unmistakable, especially on its predominantly unmade stages, as Kankkunen, seen here on his winning run in 1991, well knows.

KKK at work in a Delta Integrale during the Safari Rally of Kenya.

D 50

Lancia's foray into Formula One was but a fleeting moment in the company's long history of motor sport success: even so, it was not without satisfying results, achieved with technology which was certainly avant garde for the period. It all began way back in 1953 in the wake of the great success of the D 23 and D 24 road racers: literally a track record which convinced Gianni Lancia to also compete with his own single-seat open wheeler. The task of creating the new car was given to a man who for decades had been one of the greatest names in modern racing car design, Vittorio Jano, father of the ferocious Alfa Romeos P2 and P3. To develop his new potential winner, Jano brought together a number of innovative ideas that turned the D 50 into a real threat to the giants of the day, the Mercedes-Benz W196 and the Ferrari Supersqualo. To lower the new car's centre of gravity, provide it with outstanding roadholding and aerodynamic penetration, Jano came up with the brilliant idea of off-setting the engine at 12° to its longitudinal axis, so as to place the propellor shaft alongside the driver's seat rather than under the car. This also meant he could lower the engine and gain more space with which to create a flatter, slimmer and more aerodynamic front end as well as one which helped achieve his objective of lowering the revolutionary Lancia's centre of gravity for better roadholding. Another masterstroke was the location of the

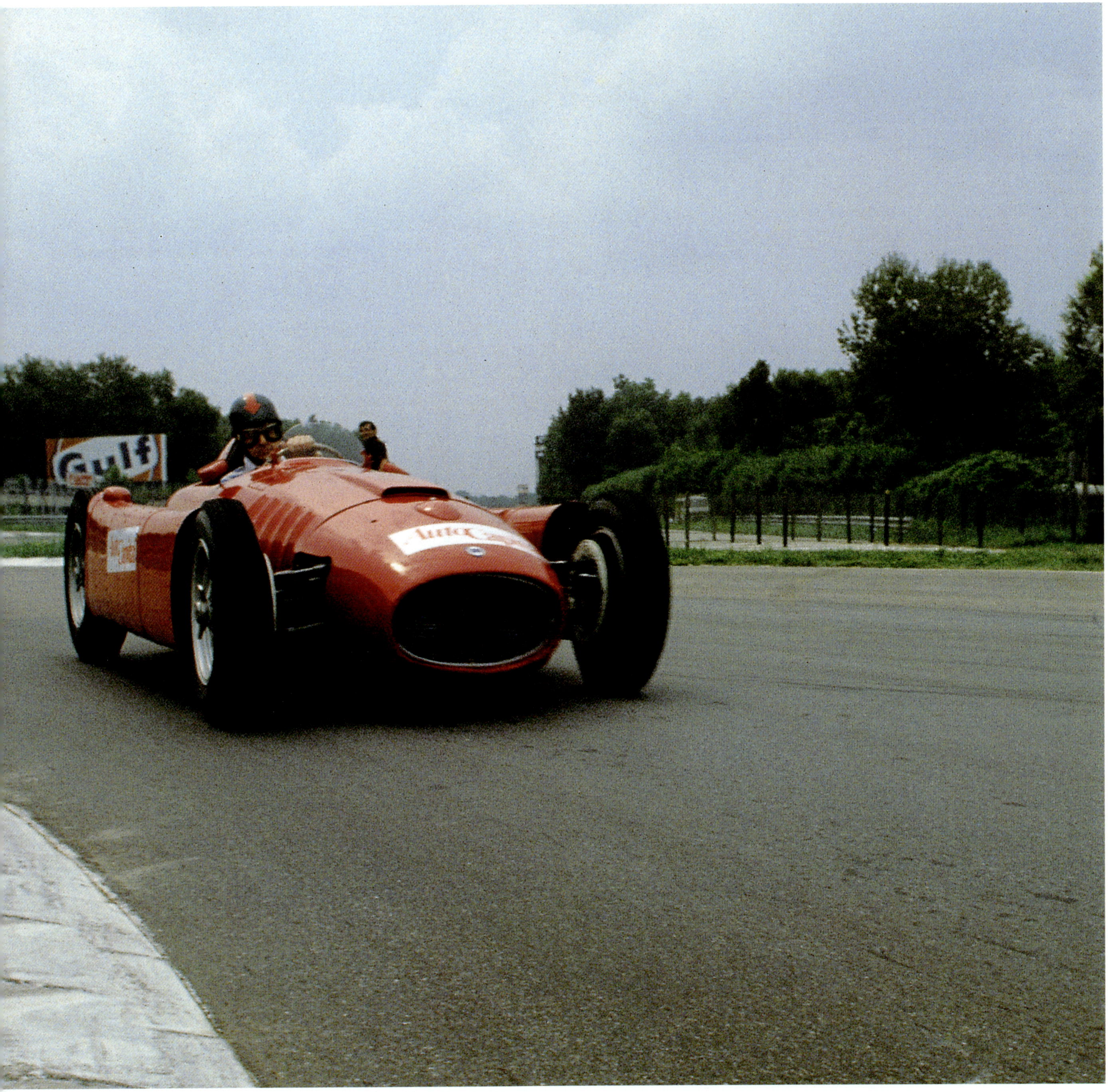
Gulf

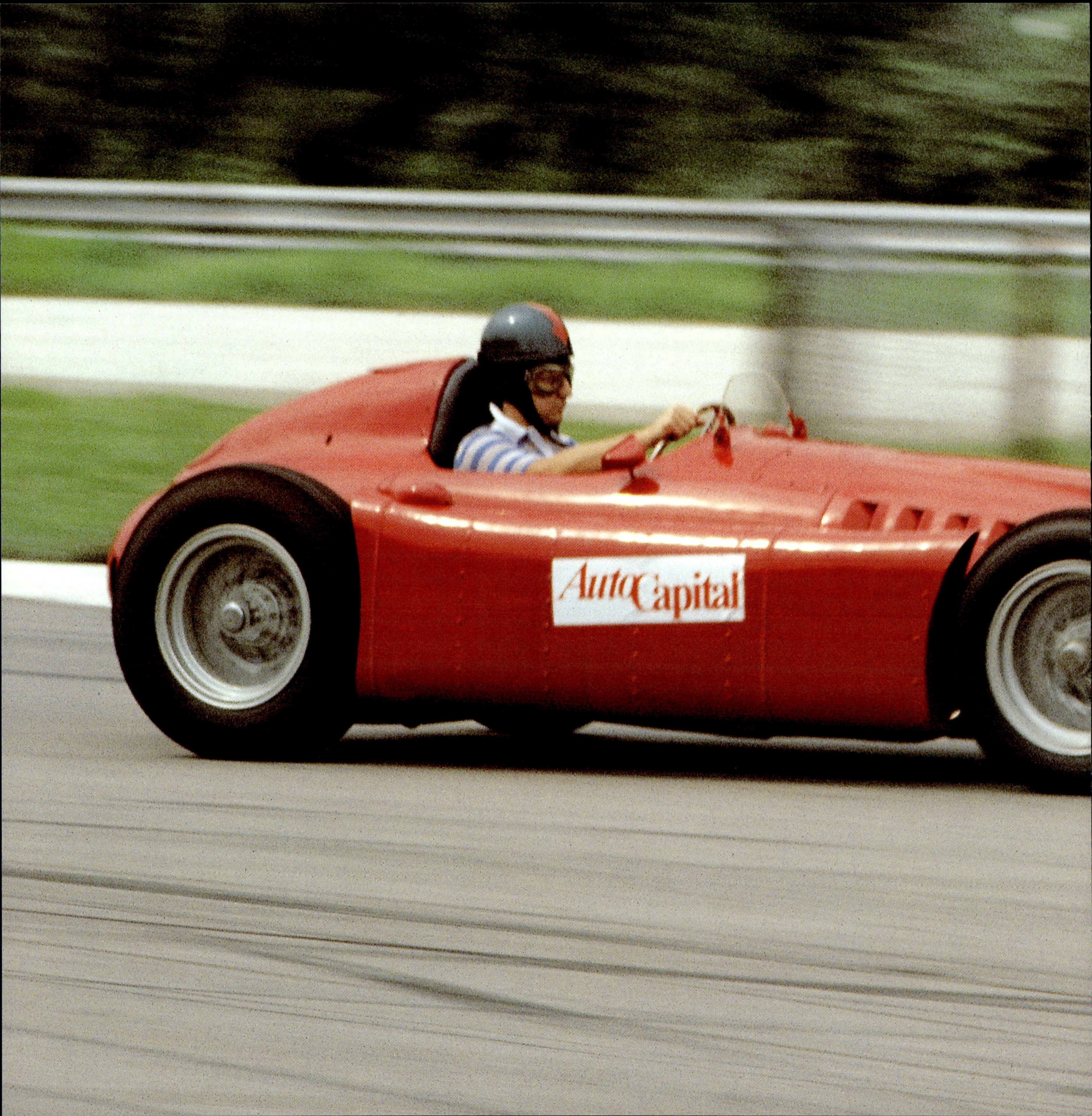
AutoCapital

gearbox in a transverse position, grouped together in one unit with the differential and multi-disc oil bath clutch: this approach ensured considerably better weight distribution on both axles to guarantee yet more grip. But that was not all. To further perfect the car's roadholding, Jano also decided to place two fuel tanks outside the car's body, one on each side of the central tub, between the two axles. As well as perfectly balancing the weight of the fuel, even when the tanks were not completely full, this innovation also created aerodynamic continuity between the front and rear wheels, further improving the car's air penetration. Another groundbreaking development was the design of the chassis, a framework of metal tubes in which the powerful 90° V8 engine played a semi-load bearing role, the front suspension anchored to its structure: this technique of using the engine as a load-bearing chassis component,

In action at Monza once again: the D 50 from the Lancia museum still shows all its aggressive speed, more than 40 years after its retirement from Formula One.

A simple hand-written inscription on the back of the driver's seat, personalised for "Mr. Villoresi": that was how Formula One was in those days.

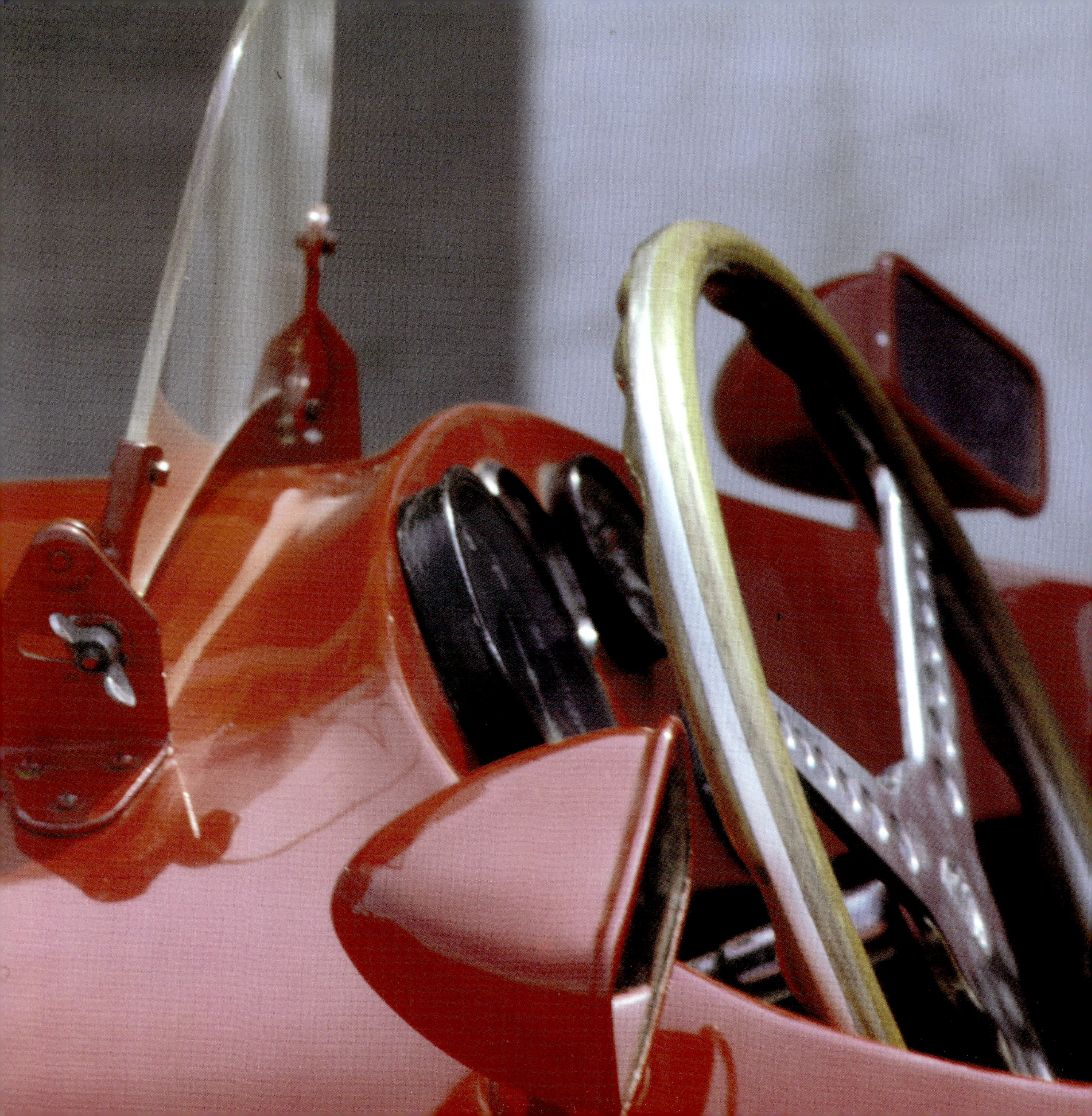

many years ahead of its time and still the basis of today's Formula One cars half a century later, was one of a whole series of epoch-making Jano developments. So to define the D 50 as revolutionary and innovative is a rather modest way of describing such a masterpiece, but it was all of those things and more. It is also true that the adoption of all those avant-garde technical solutions contributed to creating an aesthetic line for a car so that, even today, it remains one of the most alluring open wheel racers ever designed. Even compared to its opponents, the D 50 was, perhaps, the most attractive and harmonious of them all, with those beautiful fuel tanks decorating its sides and the proportional balance the car's body as a whole: to many, the D 50 was the most successful combination of F1 power, technology and beauty of its era. In its attempt to make this brilliant blend of beauty and advanced technology

Left: The large, wood-rimmed aluminium steering wheel rises maliciously above the cockpit: it was used by some of the greatest racing drivers of the Fifties.

Spoked wheels, a typical sporting symbol of those mythical years, accommodates the D 50's large brake drums.

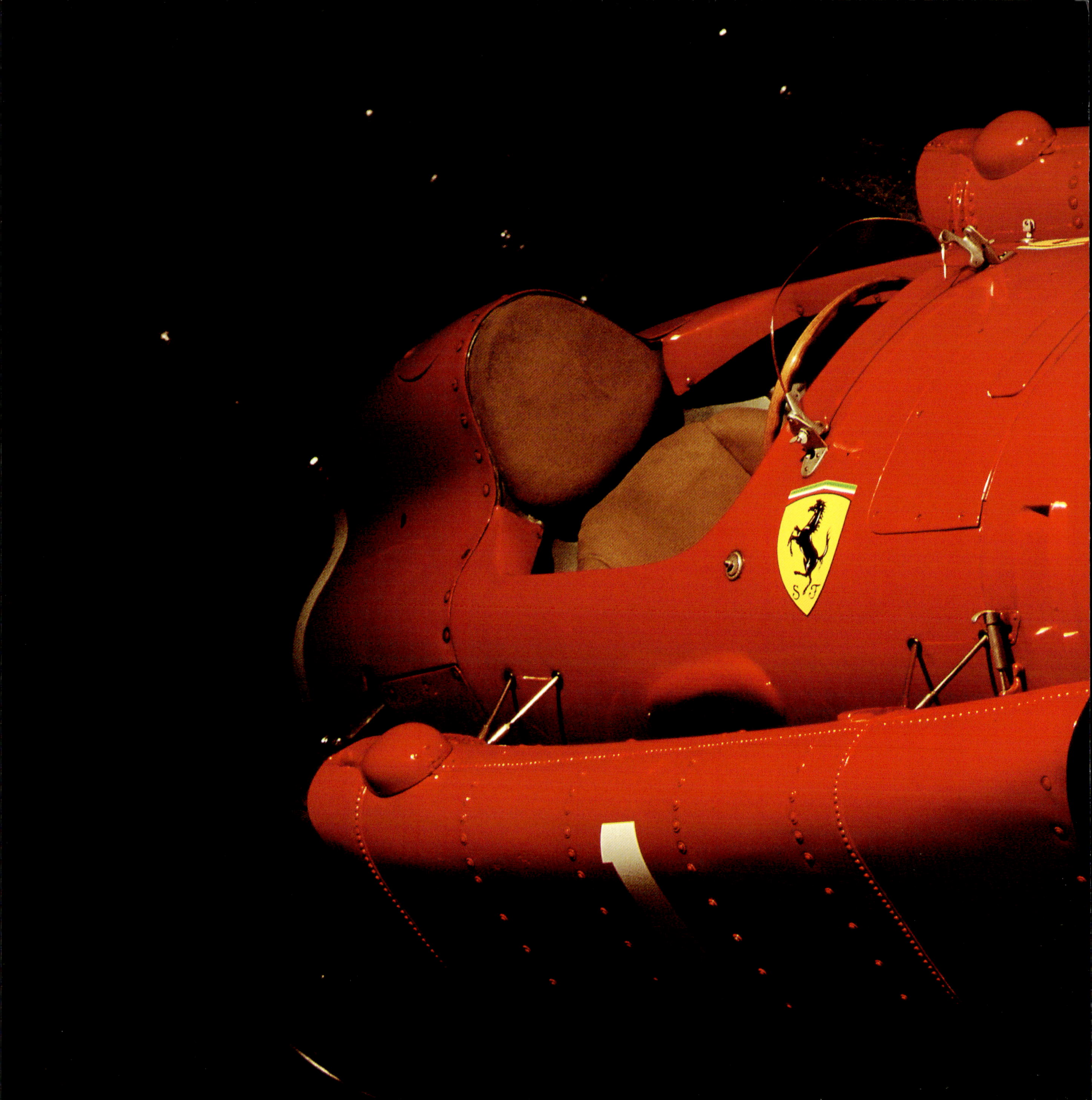

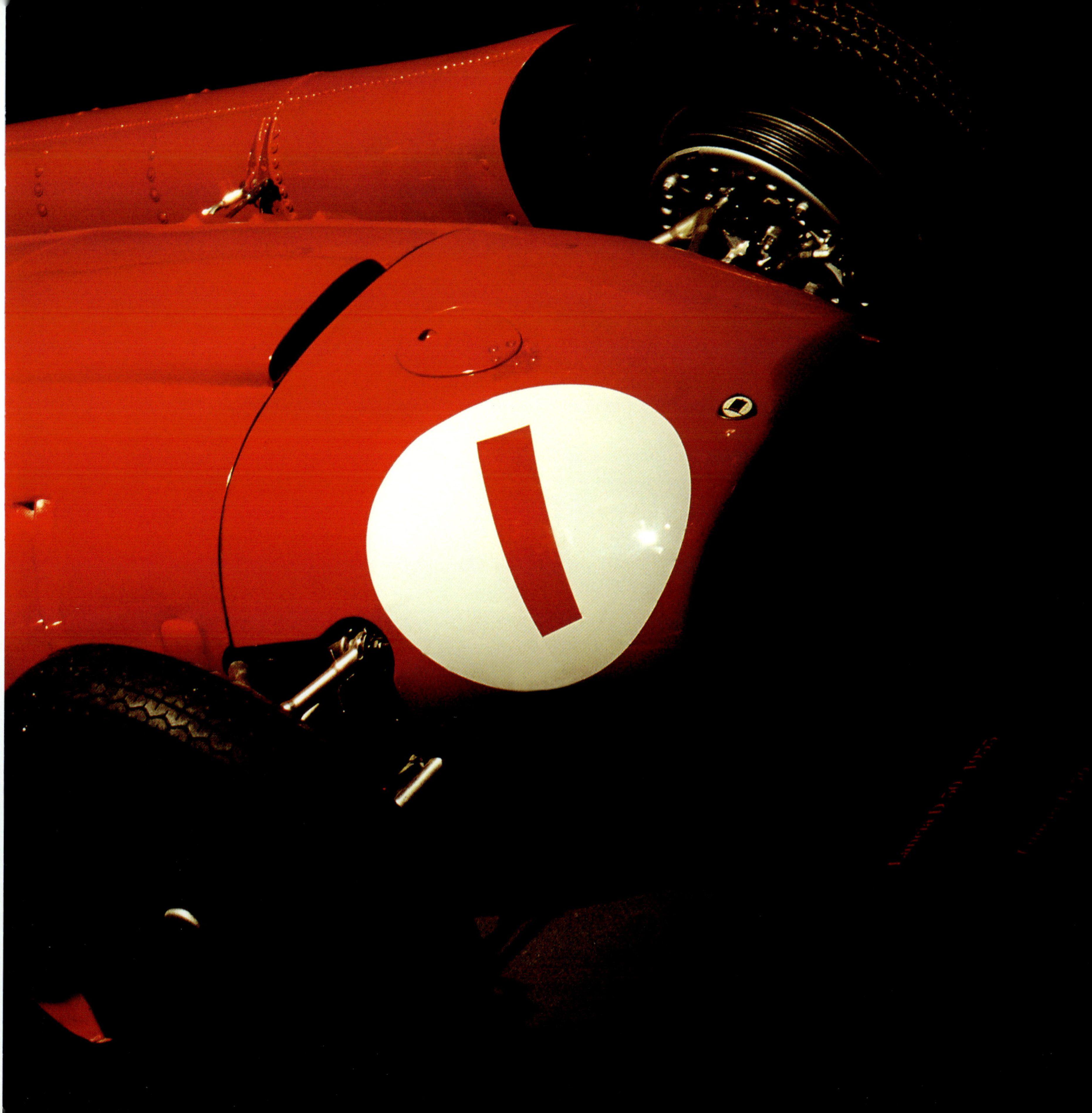

uncatchable on the tracks of the Formula One World Championship, Lancia fitted the D 50 with an equally innovative engine: a 2.5 litre eight cylinder power unit with four overhead camshafts and twin ignition (new at the time) which, back in 1953, was able to develop a remarkable 250 hp at 8000 rpm, the final version 260 hp at 8200 rpm. All these mechanical components, which also performed semi-load bearing functions within the chassis complex - a framework of tubing - attractively dressed in noble aluminium weighed a total of just 608 kg, making the D 50 the second lightest Formula One car of the period, the lightest being the 590 kg Supersqualo. Such commitment to perfection was not wasted: the results achieved by the D 50 in competition repaid with interest the tremendous efforts made by its creator. After a somewhat modest beginning, with retirements in Spain and Argentina, a D50 driven by Alberto Ascari finally scored a home win, taking first place in the Grand Prix of Turin on 27 May, 1955. Soon afterwards, the car competed in the Grand Prix of Pau, where Eugenio Castellotti drove it into second place, followed by Gigi Villoresi in fourth and Ascari in fifth. Ascari and the D 50 scored their second victory in the Circuit of Posillipo on 8 May, with Villoresi fourth.

The prancing horse first appeared on the D 50's flanks in 1956, when Scuderia Ferrari inherited six of the eight cars built by Lancia.

Beautiful and powerful, in this full frontal view the Lancia shows the clever way its fuel tanks are fixed to the sides of its body.

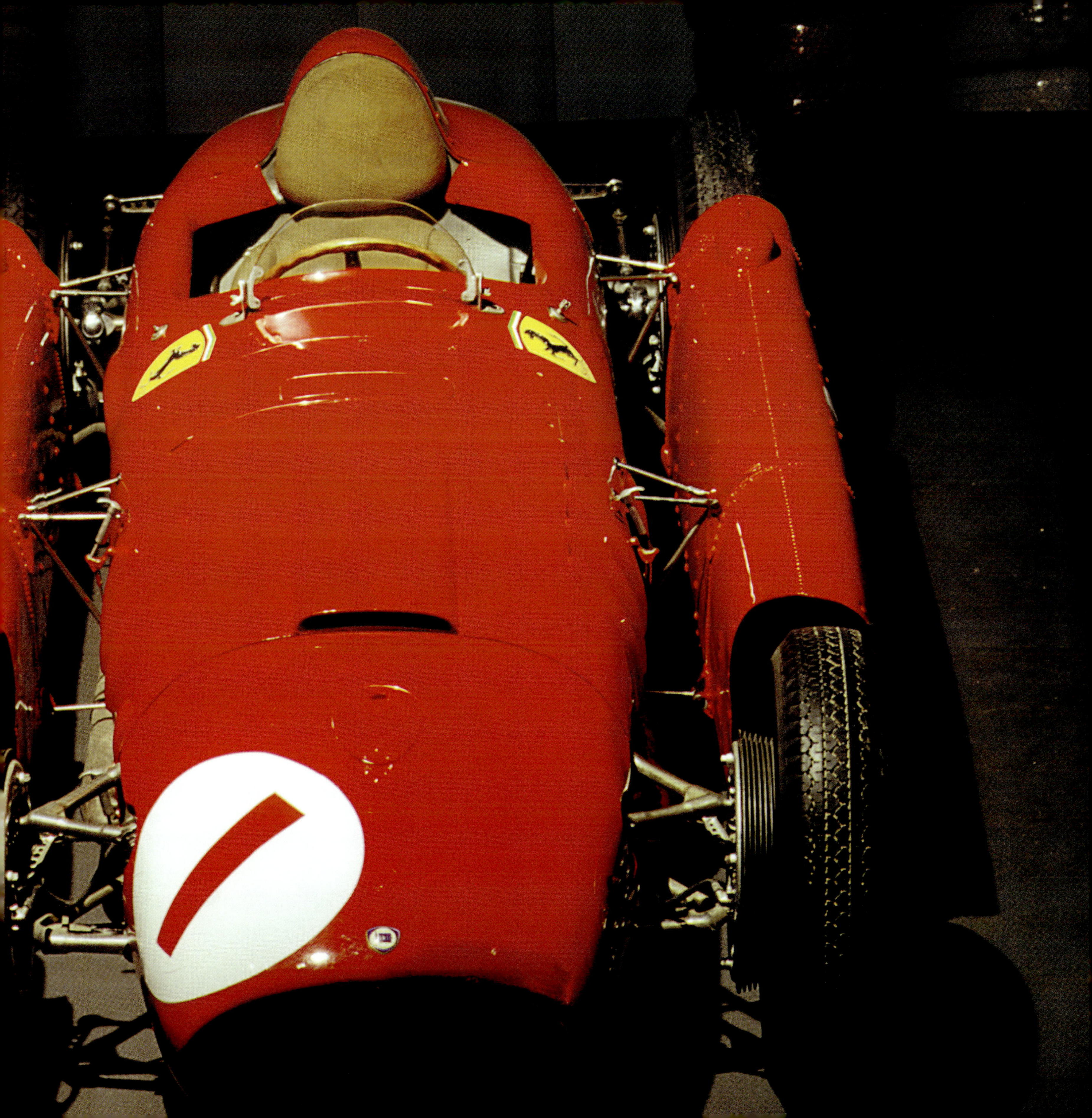

The massive brake drum and the independent front suspension with double wishbones.

track and overturned: the great champion was fatally injured. After Ascari's tragic death, the D 50 ended its racing career with the official Lancia works team. Deeply distressed by the loss of Ascari, Gianni Lancia decided to retire his cars from competition, leaving the enormous potential of this revolutionary new racer under-exploited under his company banner for reasons beyond the determination and tenacity of its creators. But the D 50's racing career did not end there: as confirmation of its avant garde technical content, six of the eight cars built by Lancia were handed over to Scuderia Ferrari under an agreement reached with Enzo Ferrari at the express request of Fiat. The Drake took charge of the cars and ensured the D 50 returned to the track branded with his famous yellow and black prancing horse shield: and it is in that livery that Juan Manuel Fangio won the 1956 Formula One World Championship at the wheel of the Jano masterpiece. A strange destiny for this beautiful single-seater, which only repaid the hard work of its creators when it belonged to another team.

The Lancia badge on the nose of the D 50 cut through the air at 186 mph (300 km/h), powered by the car's potent V8 engine.

Unlike today's crowded 16-17 race calendar, this heroic period of Formula One saw far fewer races during the year, but one of the most fascinating of them then and now is the Grand Prix of Monaco. After the promise shown by the D 50 in previous events, optimism began to build up at Lancia as the principality's race drew closer and, to go for it, Gianni Lancia decided to field four cars for the mythical event. As well as Ascari, Casatellotti and Villoresi, a fourth D 50 was assigned to Louis Chiron, who had already won the 1954 Rally of Monte Carlo for Lancia in a B 20. Having dominated the GP for 50 laps, Ascari hit a patch of oil at the chicane after exiting the tunnel and his D 50 skidded into the harbour: a true hero, the Milanese driver swam ashore uninjured. Even so, the race was not a defeat for Lancia: Castellotti took the lead but came second after a simple spin, while the remaining D 50s came fifth and sixth. But destiny had already shown its hand. Four days later at Monza, Ascari climbed aboard a racing car for the last time, a Ferrari Sport. Another underpass, another bend (now named after him) but this time, the car left the

129

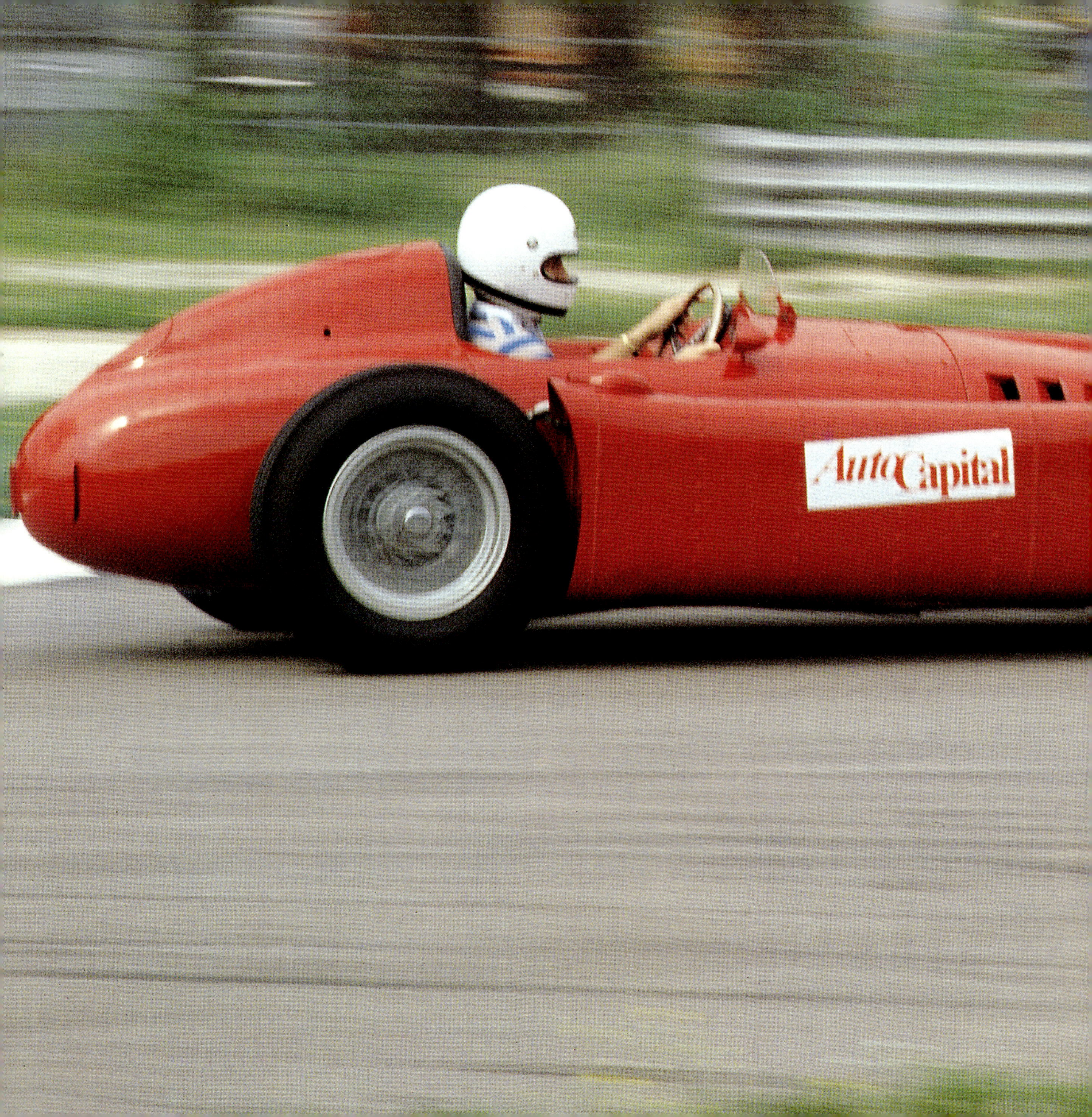
AutoCapital

Technical specifications of the D 50

ENGINE: 90° V8
ENGINE POSITION: front, inclined at 12° to the longitudinal axis
CUBIC CAPACITY: 2488 cc (second series 2485.9 cc, third series 2480 cc)
BORE AND STROKE: 73.6x73.1 mm (second series 76x68.2 mm, third series 74x72 mm)
DISTRIBUTION: twin chain-driven overhead camshafts per cylinder bank
NUMBER OF VALVES: two per cylinder
COMPRESSION RATIO: 10.5:1
FUEL SUPPLY: four twin-choke Solex 40 P11 carburettors in inverted position
IGNITION: double, with coil and distributor and two spark plugs per cylinder
COOLING: liquid, front radiator
MAXIMUM POWER: 250 hp at 8000 rpm (second series 255 hp at 8000 rpm, third series 260 hp at 8200 rpm)
MAXIMUM TORQUE: 23.2 kg/m at 4000 rpm
BODY: single-seater in aluminium
CHASSIS: tubular monocoque with semi-load bearing engine
SUSPENSION: independent front, superimposed wishbones, transverse semi-eliptic springs, anti-roll bar, hydraulic telescopic shock absorbers; De Dion rear axle with reaction struts and anchoring forked rod, transverse lower semi-eliptic springs, hydraulic telescopic shock absorbers
TRANSMISSION: rear mounted five-speed gearbox with reverse, en bloc with differential and clutch
CLUTCH: multi-disc, oil bath
BRAKES: hydraulically operated drums front and rear
DIMENSIONS: length 3330 mm (second version 3360 mm), width 1540 mm, height 920 mm
WHEELBASE AND TRACK: 2485 mm (third version 2480 mm); front 1294 mm, rear 1330 mm
TYRES: 5.50-16 front, 7.00-16 rear
DRY WEIGHT: 608 kg
PERFORMANCE: maximum speed 186 mph (with long ratios)

A symbolic step back into the past aboard a D 50 which, powering into today's Serraglio corner at Monza, finds the Lancia of Juan Manuel Fangio on its way to winning the 1956 Grand Prix of Great Britain.

133

D 25

In the wake of the success of the D 20, D 23 and D 24 and with an inevitable technological push from the preceding D 50 Formula One project, the highly advanced D 25 first saw the light of day in the Lancia racing department in Turin. This fabulous barchetta open-top racing car and its sinuous, tapered body in noble aluminium resembled the D 50 much more than its predecessors, despite its closed wheels: and the D 25 boasted some of the technological innovations pioneered by its exotic Formula One sibling, including an en bloc single gearbox, clutch and differential, the modern monocoq steel tube chassis in chromomolybdenum and suspension with De Dion rear axle. Like the D 50, the D 25 was the brainchild of the great Vittorio Jano, who brought so many innovations to motor racing in more than three decades of groundbreaking work. As did the D 50 in Formula One, the new barchetta was to represent the pinnacle of Lancia's involvement in sports car racing, perpetuating the successes of its predecessors in the category: in reality, though, it had a brief motor racing career and did not achieve the results expected of it, although this was also due to the awkward period into which it was born. At the time, Lancia was investing heavily in Formula One which, perhaps, overshadowed the stupendous D 25: the car brought to a close a glorious period in the company's sporting history, which harked back to the D 20, the first six cylinder twin overhead cam engined Lancia. The fabulous D 20 coupé

135

The beautiful profile of this tapering coupé is broken only by the outline of its vertical windscreen.

The hump, which begins as the driver's headrest, is a typical aerodynamic and aesthetic component of the distant Fifties.

The Plexiglas cover of the headlight distinguished even more the period's final and most advanced version of the open-top Lancia from its sister car, the D 24.

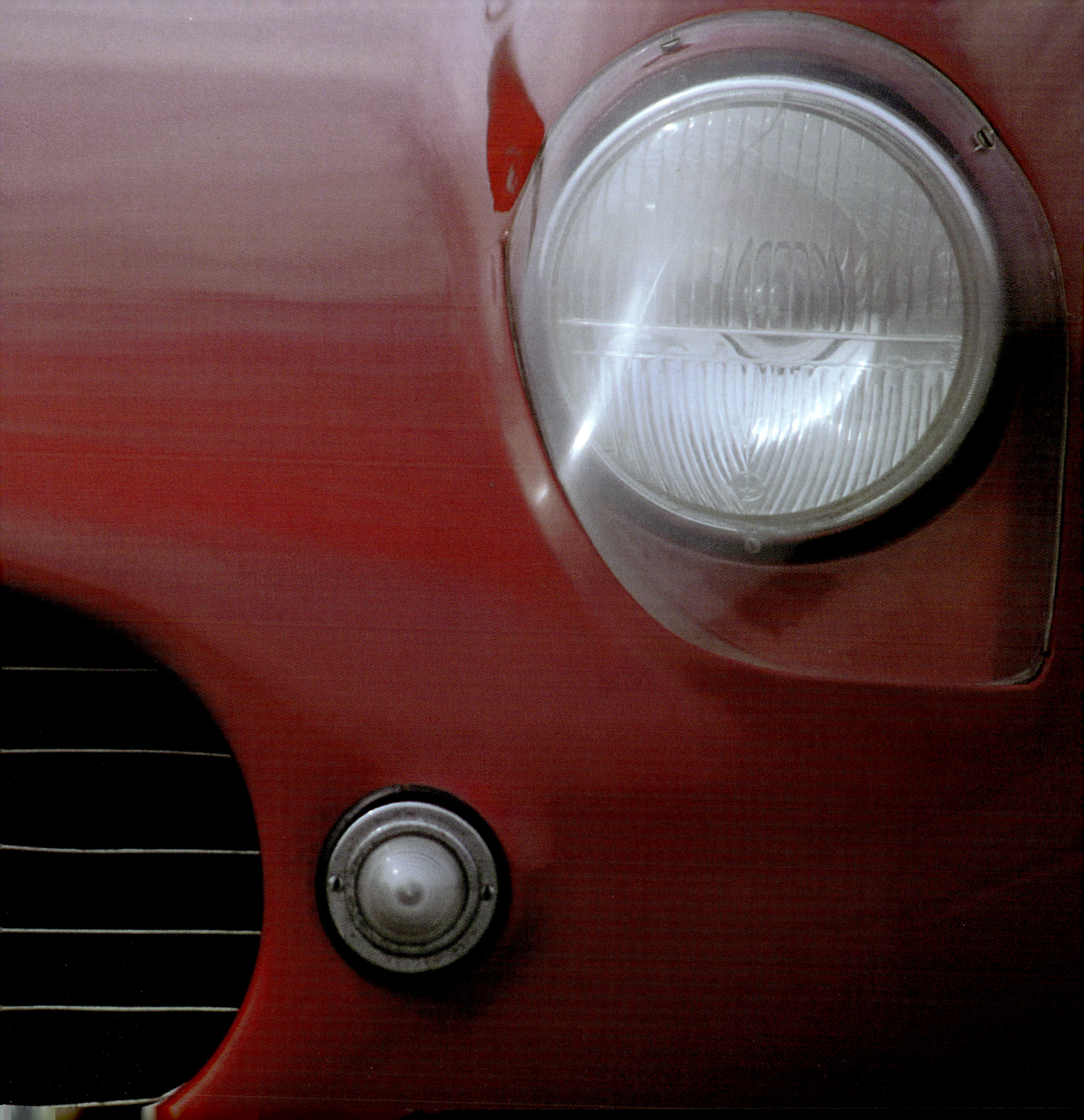

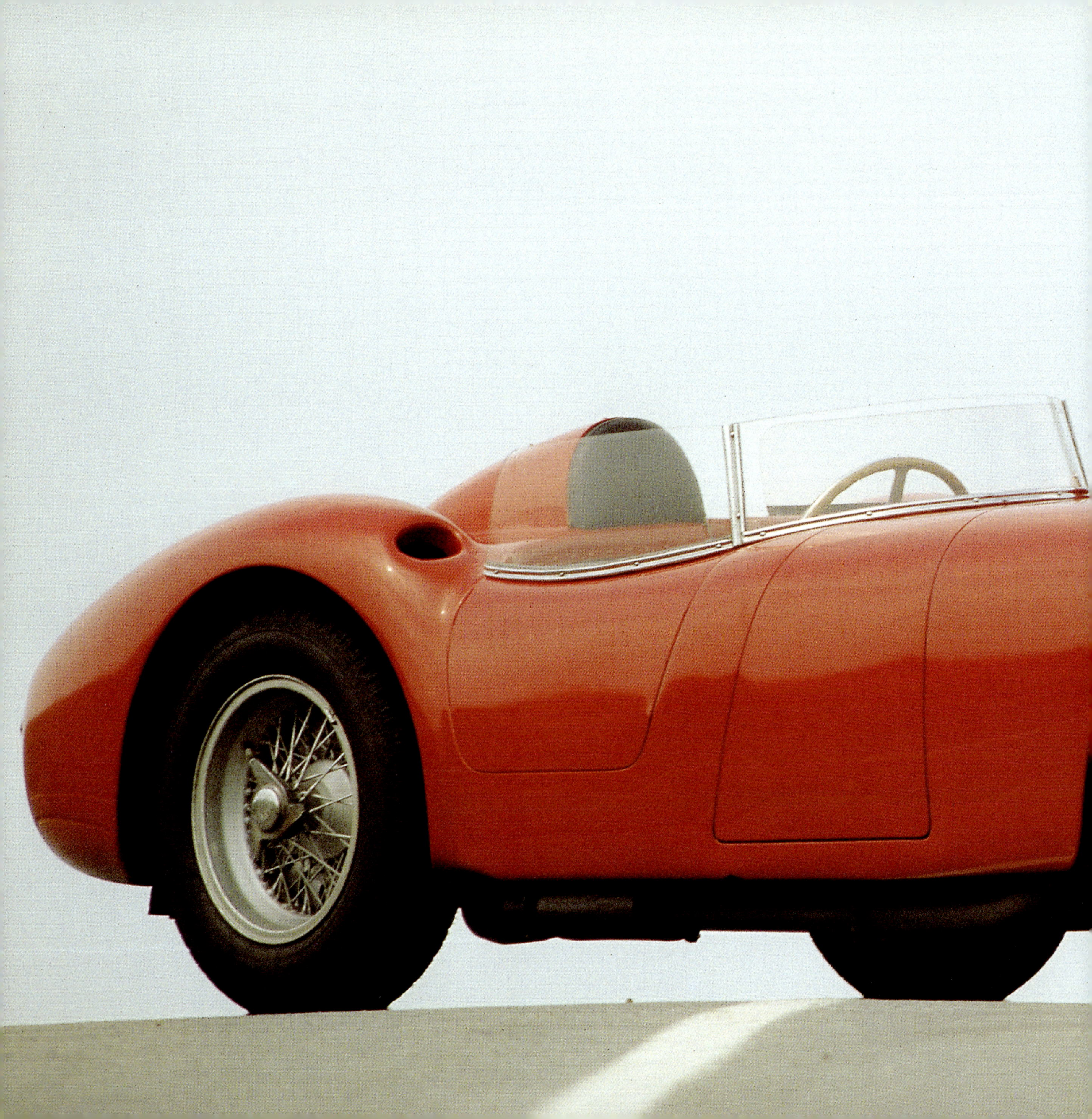

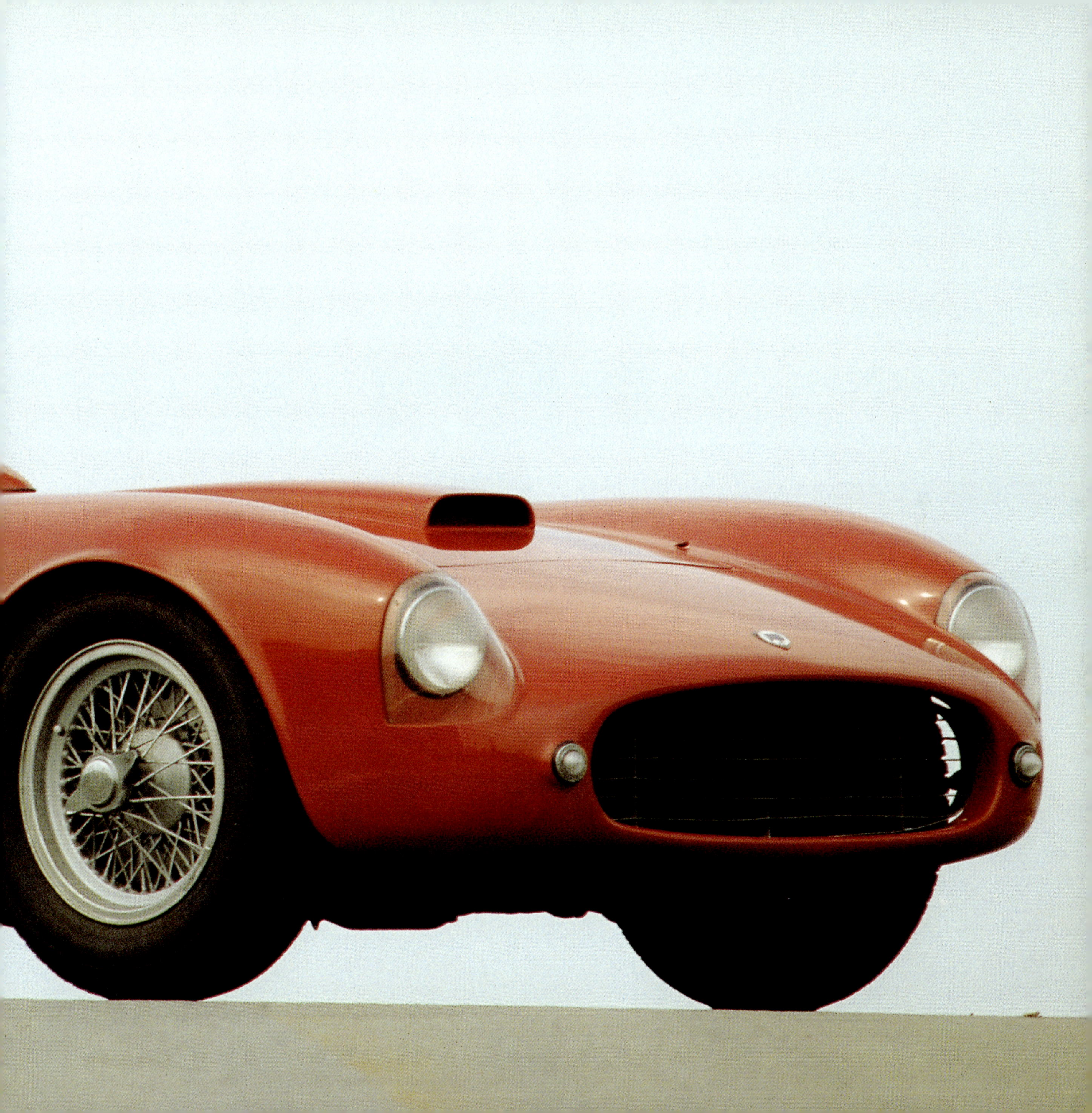

scored its first major victory soon after its debut, in the hands of Umberto Maglioli in the 1953 Targa Florio. To test the D 20 in competition for the first time before the big race, Maglioli drove the coupé in the minor Palermo-Monte Pellegrino event – and won. The car, predecessor of the D 25, raced in Lancia's old colours: after that, though, the sky blue and yellow livery remained a distant memory until Cesare Fiorio had it dusted off and used again on the cylinder head of the glorious Fulvia HF. The D 25 was fitted with a 65° V6, 3750 cc engine that produced a massive 305 hp at 6500 rpm to give the long ratio version a top speed of almost 186 mph (300 km/h), remarkable for almost 50 years ago. All of which made the D 25 one of the most advanced and highest performance cars in its category. A lightweight, too, weighing in at just 755 kg due to the aluminium that "dressed" the advanced chromo molybdenum frame, a further performance guarantee which also improved the car's road holding. If one considers that, way back in 1954, this car enjoyed a power to weight ratio of less than 2.5 kilos being pulled along the road by each unit of horse power, it is easy to see how its performance was comparable to that of the latest open top sports cars on today's roads, which are unlikely to dip below 2.7 k/hp. The D 25's front suspension system comprised superimposed wishbones and leafsprings and De Dion axle with leafsprings at the rear. It was probably the car's wheelbase, a trifle long for this type of sports car, which was its only negative factor for it made the car less agile (there was also a 2300 mm short wheelbase version). More than 40 years after its debut and following meticulous restoration, the splendid D 25 pictured in this book has twice taken part in the Mille Miglia Storica, crossing the finish line unscathed and not far down the leader board, driven by Gino Valenzano the first year and Claudio Maglioli in 1989. The two drivers said the only problem they experienced was in braking on fast sections, which cannot be the same with a Fifties racer as it is with the hi-tech packages we use today for routine transport. The D 25 was the final evolution of the Lancia racing car family of its period: to see a works Lancia in international competition again we had to wait for the HF works team created by Cesare Fiorio, who would take the Lancia Flavia Coupé racing eight years later and, after that, the Fulvia.

The front end cut through the air with its tapered shape, while the large oval grill allowed the engine to breathe.

The convex rear wing enabled the shape of the flanks to remain low.

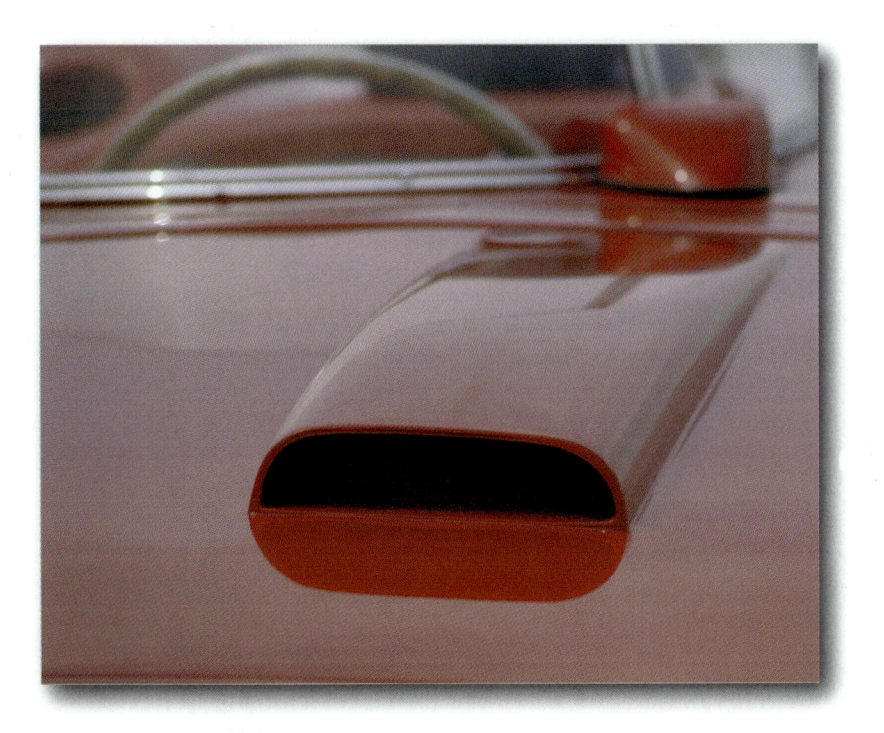

The potent V6 engine of the D 25 also took breath through the large air intake on the car's bonnet. The engine produced 305 hp in 1954: with a top speed of almost 186 mph (300 km/h), all ordinary mortals usually saw of the car was its disappearing rear end.

The passenger seat was hidden under an aluminium tonneau cover, which improved aerodynamics.

The perfect harmony of the car's beautiful lines delineates the gorgeous aluminium body, which was hand shaped as was the practice in the Fifties.

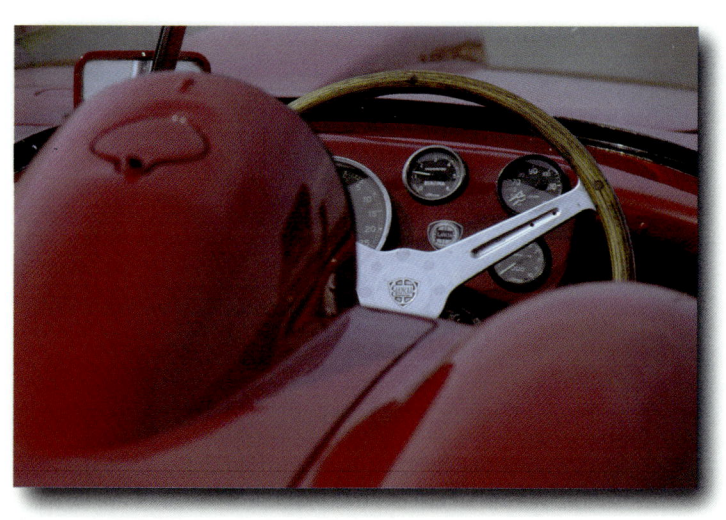

Among the rounded shapes of the body, the star was the beautiful three-spoke steering wheel, with its wooden rim that framed the instruments.

The power unit of the D 25 also had a pleasant aesthetic appearance: the cylinder heads are beautiful mechanical sculptures.

The rev counter on the left makes space for a Lancia shield between the dials.

The vertical windscreen delineates the cockpit and leaves space for the brakes' air intake in the rear wing.

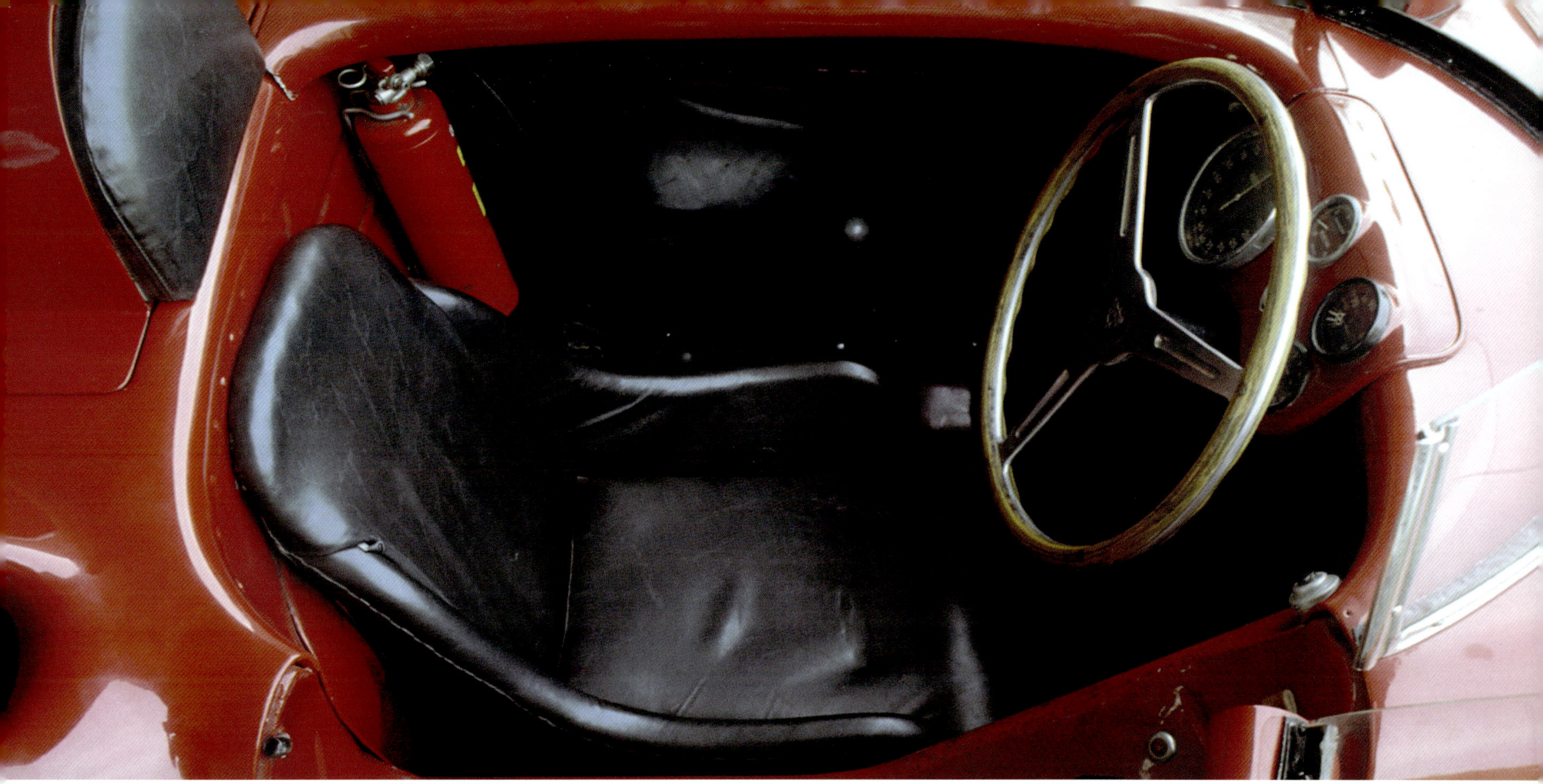

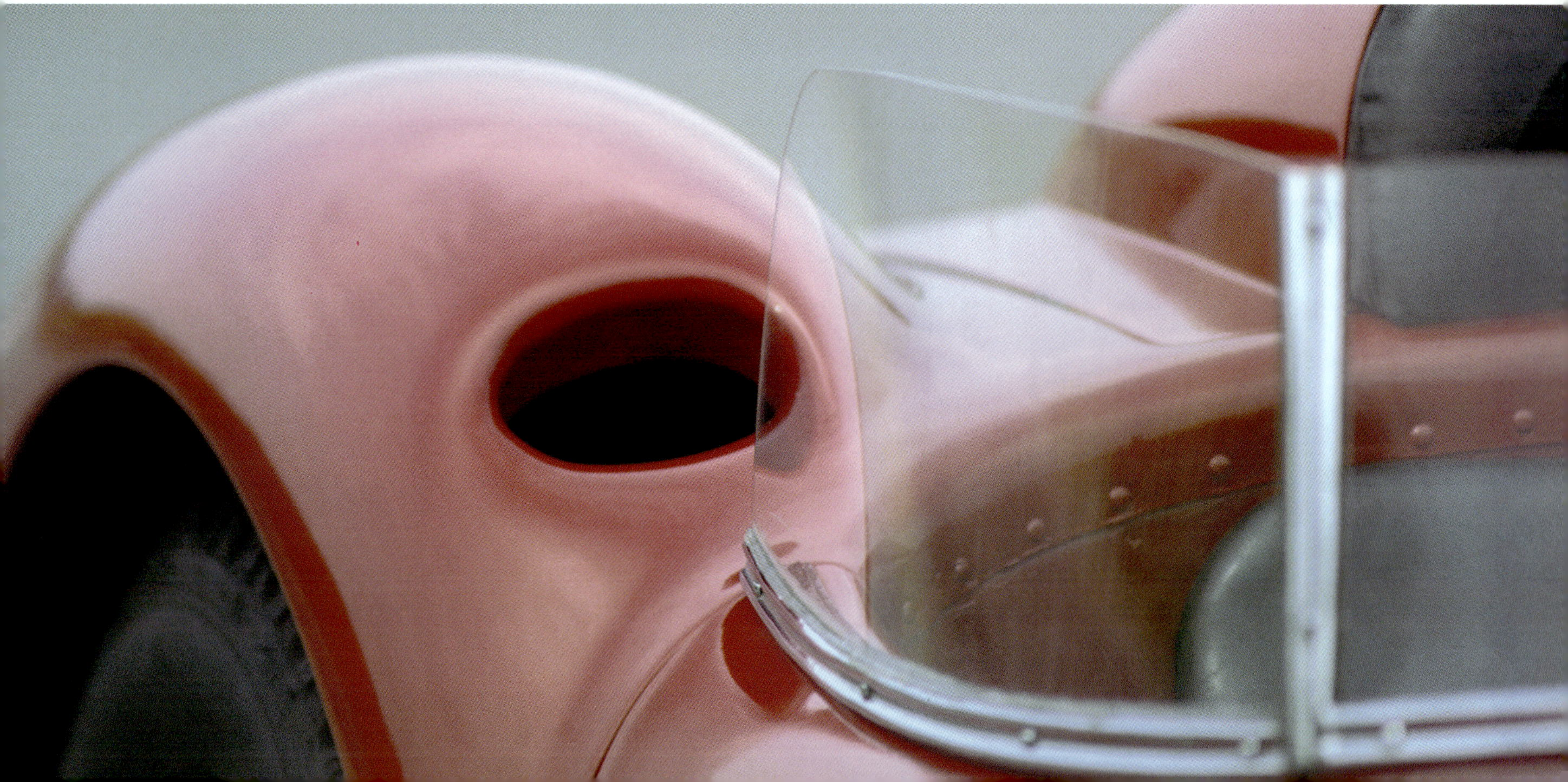

Technical specifications of the D 25

ENGINE: V6 set at 60°
ENGINE POSITION: front, longitudinal
CUBIC CAPACITY: 3750 cc
STROKE AND BORE: 93x92 mm
DISTRIBUTION: twin overhead chain-driven camshafts per cylinder bank
NUMBER OF VALVES: two per cylinder
COMPRESSION RATIO: 9:1
FUEL SYSTEM: three Weber 46 DCF 3 carburettors
IGNITION: double distributor, two spark plugs per cylinder
COOLING: liquid, front radiator
MAXIMUM POWER: 305 hp at 6500 rpm
BODY: open-top two-seater, aluminium body
CHASSIS: framework of tubes in chromomolybdenum
SUSPENSION: front superimposed wishbones, De Dion rear axle with leaf springs and stabiliser bar
TRANSMISSION: rear-wheel drive, four-speed gearbox with reverse, en block with clutch and differential
CLUTCH: dry mono-disc
BRAKES: drums front and rear
DIMENSIONS: length 3800 mm, width 1440 mm, height 960 mm
WHEELBASE AND TRACK: 2450 mm (first version 2300 mm); front 1300 mm, rear 1300 mm (first version 1260 mm)
TYRES: Pirelli Stelvio – front 6.00x16, rear 7.00x16
PERFORMANCE: maximum speed 186 mph (300 km/h) with long gear ratios

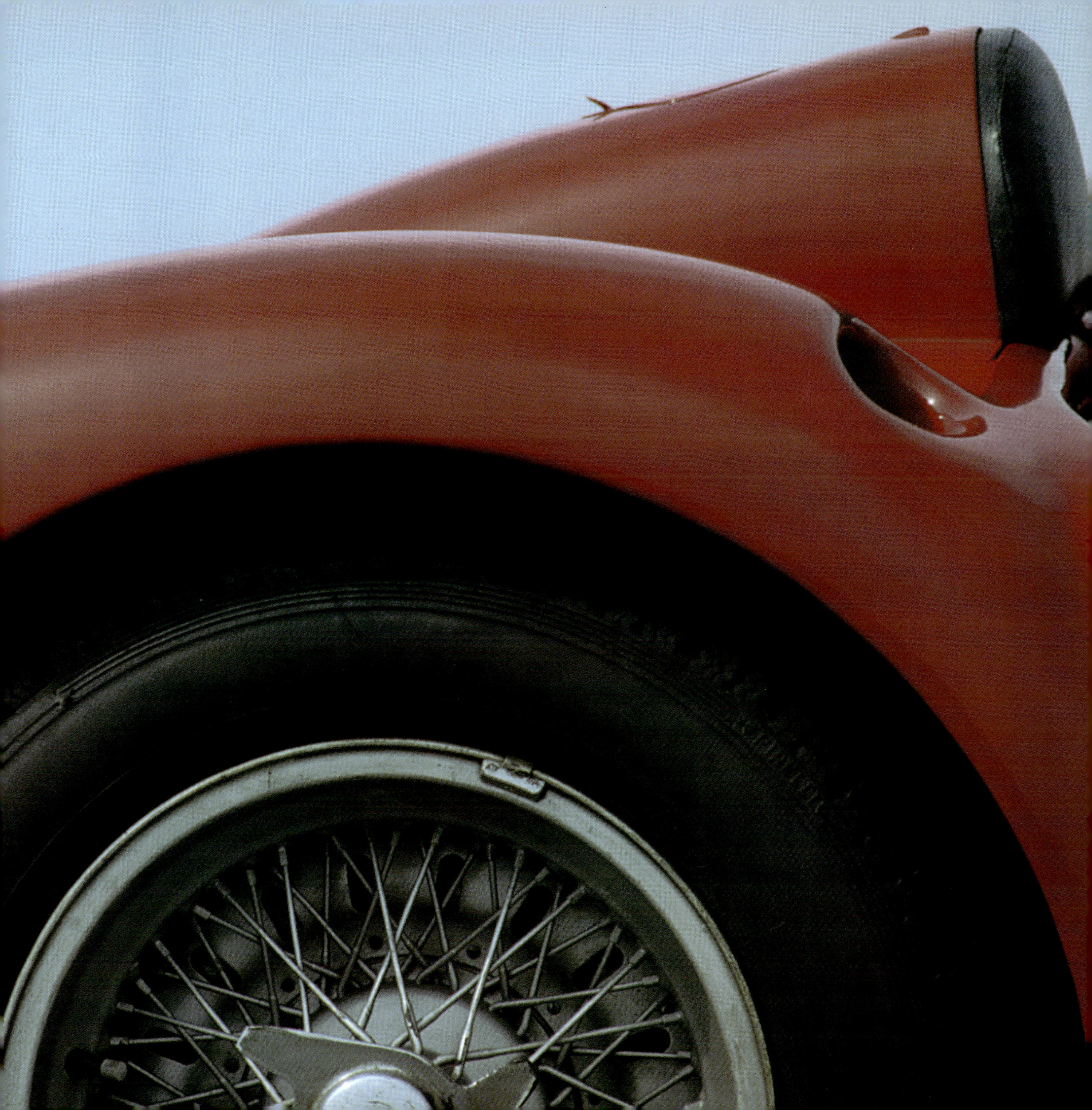

The photographs is published by courtesy of Lancia's Historic Archive.

The D 25 "watches" its closed-bodied D 20 predecessor with admiration as the older car approaches a corner at speed and eventually wins the 1953 Targa Florio.

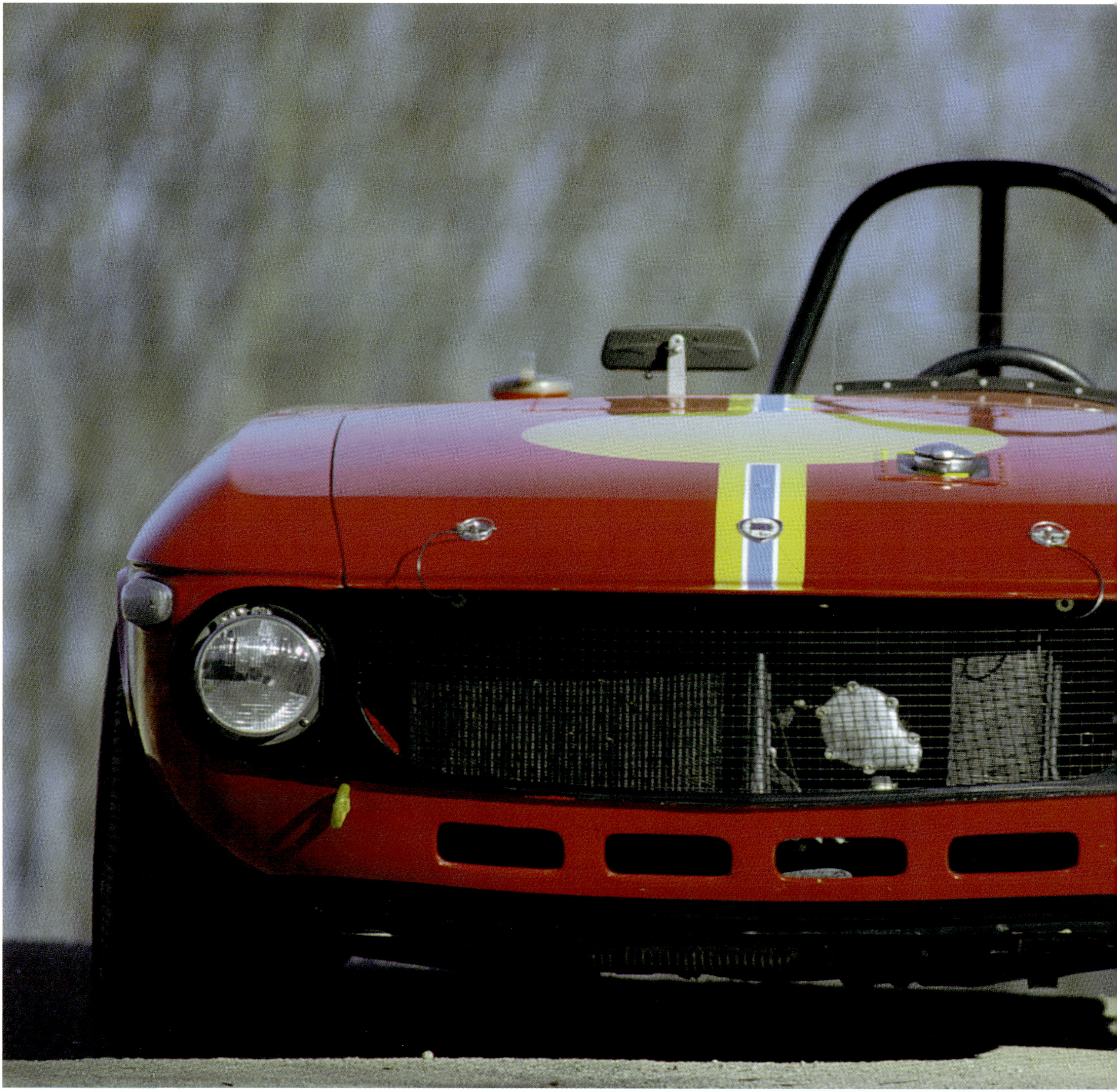

F&M SPECIAL

Born in flight from an idea linked to high temperature ... not mechanical but inside the original car's cockpit. The open-top Fulvia F&M Special is, in fact, the result of a successful idea devised by Claudio Maglioli. He was returning to Milan after having driven a Fulvia Zagato prototype in the 1969 24 Hours of Daytona and told Cesare Fiorio of the enormous discomfort caused by the heat inside the uncomfortable little coupé. "Why don't we produce an open-top car for the Targa Florio"? Maglioli asked. Soon after returning to his Turin office, Fiorio decided this new idea could work: a day later, the Lancia motor sport boss telephoned his approval of the project to Maglioli and arranged to send the Biella car tuner a Fulvia bodyshell to "uncover". There was not much time left to prepare an open-top Fulvia for the Sicilian classic and Maglioli, who was keen to see his idea come to life, literally did everything he could to build a competitive car quickly: 50 days later, the prototype Fulvia F&M Special uttered its first engine note. The constructional logic of this basic barchetta was, obviously, much improved ventilation and containment of the car's weight in favour of a considerable improvement in its power to weight ratio and the Fulvia 1300's performance. Much attention was paid to reliability on the basis that "everything that's not there can't break". Around its 150 hp engine, the barchetta's body lost all its "frills". First, the whole roof was removed; the glass windscreen went and in its place came a much smaller lower, lighter screen in Plexiglas. Inside, which had by this time become the outside, the interior was stripped; the dashboard became a simple aluminium panel with just three instruments - rev counter, water temperature gauge and ammeter; the seats were substituted by lighter, more wrap-around Ricaros and the metal pedals by others in perforated aluminium. Bonnet and boot lid were in aluminium, the bonnet air intake disappeared, while the doors were "emptied" and given nylon straps, which took the place of metal handles. The rear overhang was reduced by 28 centimetres, creating a new tail shape that became more compact and convergent: this expedient not only contributed to a maximum reduction in weight, it also slightly improved roadholding by reducing the load on the rear axle. Having stripped

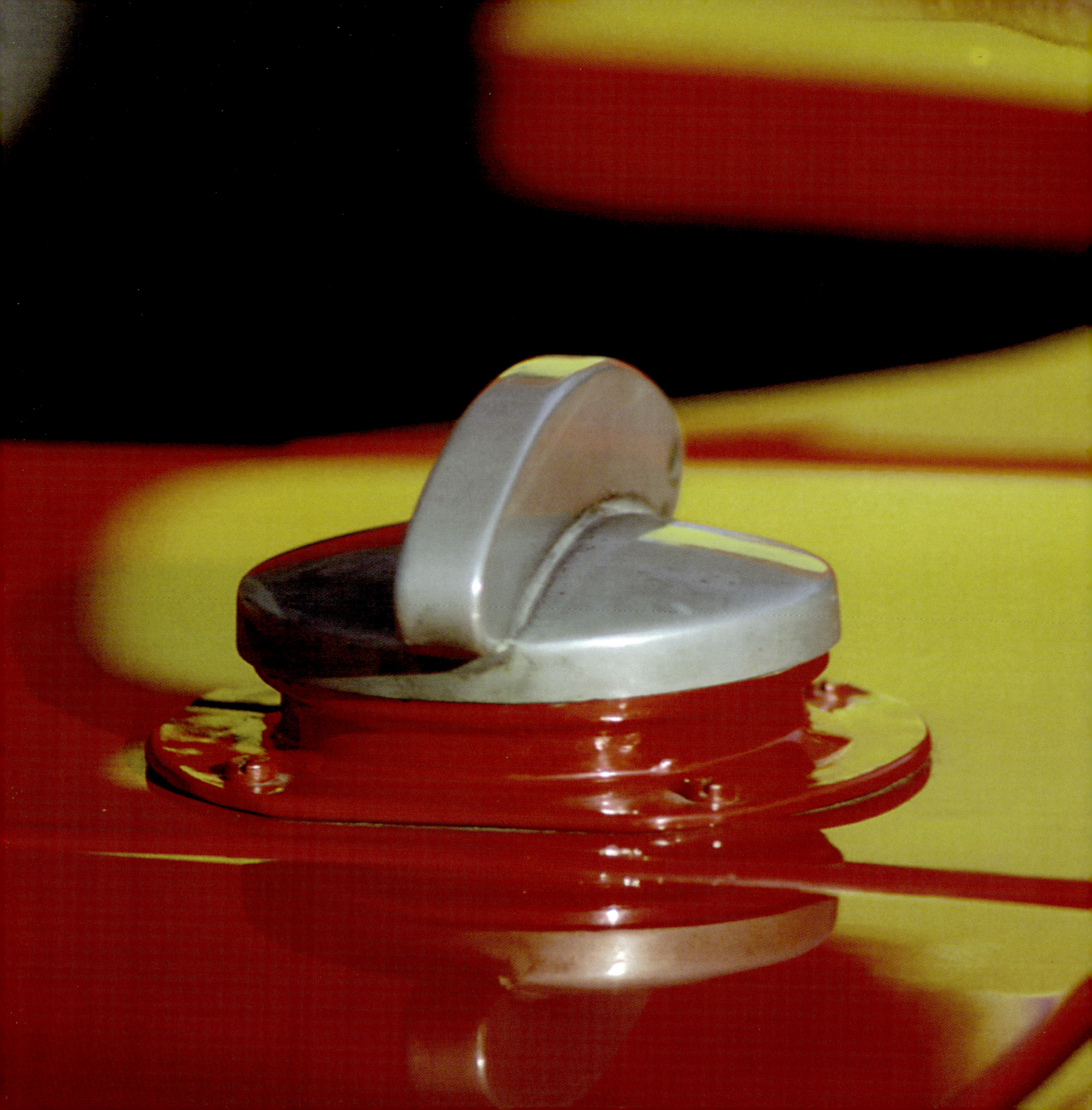

No frills, just the bare essentials to reduce weight and improve performance: that is the F&M Special.

the body of its roof and pillars, it was obviously necessary to strengthen the chassis to guarantee essential torsional rigidity: so a tubular under-chassis was built to the maximum height allowed by the rules, which sustained the lower part of the car; and a 98 litre L-shaped aluminium fuel tank was built into the boot. All of these modifications aimed at reducing weight provoked a collateral effect: a strange increase in the height of the car which, when all modifications were completed, gave the Special a ground height similar to that of a Safari Rally car! Designed to support a much greater weight, the normal production, underloaded suspension raised the body by almost 10 centimetres, compared to the road car. So it was necessary to lower the springs and suspension until the barchetta locked into its correct set-up. The F&M Special finally made its first public appearance with style in the Occhieppo-Graglia Santuario hillclimb in April, 1969: after clocking second fastest time behind a powerful Abarth 2000, Claudio Maglioli won the event the next day in driving rain. Not bad for a debut! Less than 24 hours later, Cesare Fiorio called Maglioli again, this time to ask him to build another F&M Special for the Targa Florio, which was just 10 days away! The Biella tuner pulled off that miracle, too: he put together a close-knit group of people able to draw on their experience

Left: A play of reflected light on the boot lid even makes the aluminium fuel cap look like a real work of art.

151

The enormous roll bar juts like a cupola from the squat shape of the F&M: the rear end of the Fulvia is still easily recognisable.

in building the first car. They worked day and night on the body shell of a prototype previously used by Harry Kallstrom (which would have been the standard-bearer of the Fanalone) and had the car ready just in time for it to start the Sicilian classic road race. Maglioli should have tested the F&M Special in Sicily but time was so short the second car still wore the radiator grill of the original prototype coupé from which it was derived, including its trademark two big headlamps which were later adopted for the future Fulvia Coupé Rallye 1.6. So two F&M Specials went to the Targa Florio start line, one driven by Sandro Munari and Rauno Altonen and the other by Claudio Maglioli and Raffaele Pinto. The Munari-Altonen car came ninth overall behind much more powerful and established machinery, while the Maglioli-Pinto car, which had been hot on the heels of Munari's racer, retired due to overheating caused by a page of a newspaper which had, by chance, spread itself over the barchetta's radiator grill. The racing career of the F&M Special continued at the Nürburgring, where the two cars of Munari and Pinto led the event for a considerable time before a tyre on each one punctured. The door of Pinto's car also flew open during the race so he had to stop and have it sealed. In the end, Munari and Pinto in their two Lancia lightweights still came first and second respectively in their class. After a race at Mugello, in which Munari came eighth and Maglioli 15th, the car driven by Munari was subjected to an inverted operation: as the vehicle was going to compete in the Tour de Corse rally, an event often plagued by rain and fog, a normal production glass wind-

The oil filler cap gives a real racing feel to the barchetta.

The headlight and indicator are the same as those fitted to the production Fulvia, but the big light no longer had the original chrome surround for weight reasons.

screen and rudimentary aluminium roof were added. The original weight reduction objective was dropped and the barchetta was transformed into a hybrid; as a result, it lost its fundamental advantages of spartanism and much improved handling. Following that brief, not very lucrative transformation, the two prototype open tops were pensioned off (the second was sold to a Sicilian driver, who raced it in a local championship) to make way for what would have been the F&M 2. This car did not have much in common with the look of the Fulvia either but, exploiting experience gained with the first barchetta, it was faster and more competitive: in a hillclimb like the Occhieppo-Graglia Santuario, the Mark II was 10 seconds faster over the four minute ascent than the Mark I. In reality though, the last open-top Fulvia took part in few races and did not last long as a member of the Lancia family. The Turin-based company no longer had the kind of enthusiasm which encouraged it to compete with the first two F&M Specials, particularly because the appearance of this new car did not have the "Fulvia corporate look": it did little to promote the sales of the road car, usually one of the reasons for competing in motor racing.

Even the rear view mirror was rudimentary: it was held in place by a simple aluminium stem.

An unusual, extremely dramatic perspective, comprising a number of elements of the F&M: the yellow number disc, roll bar and the large HF.

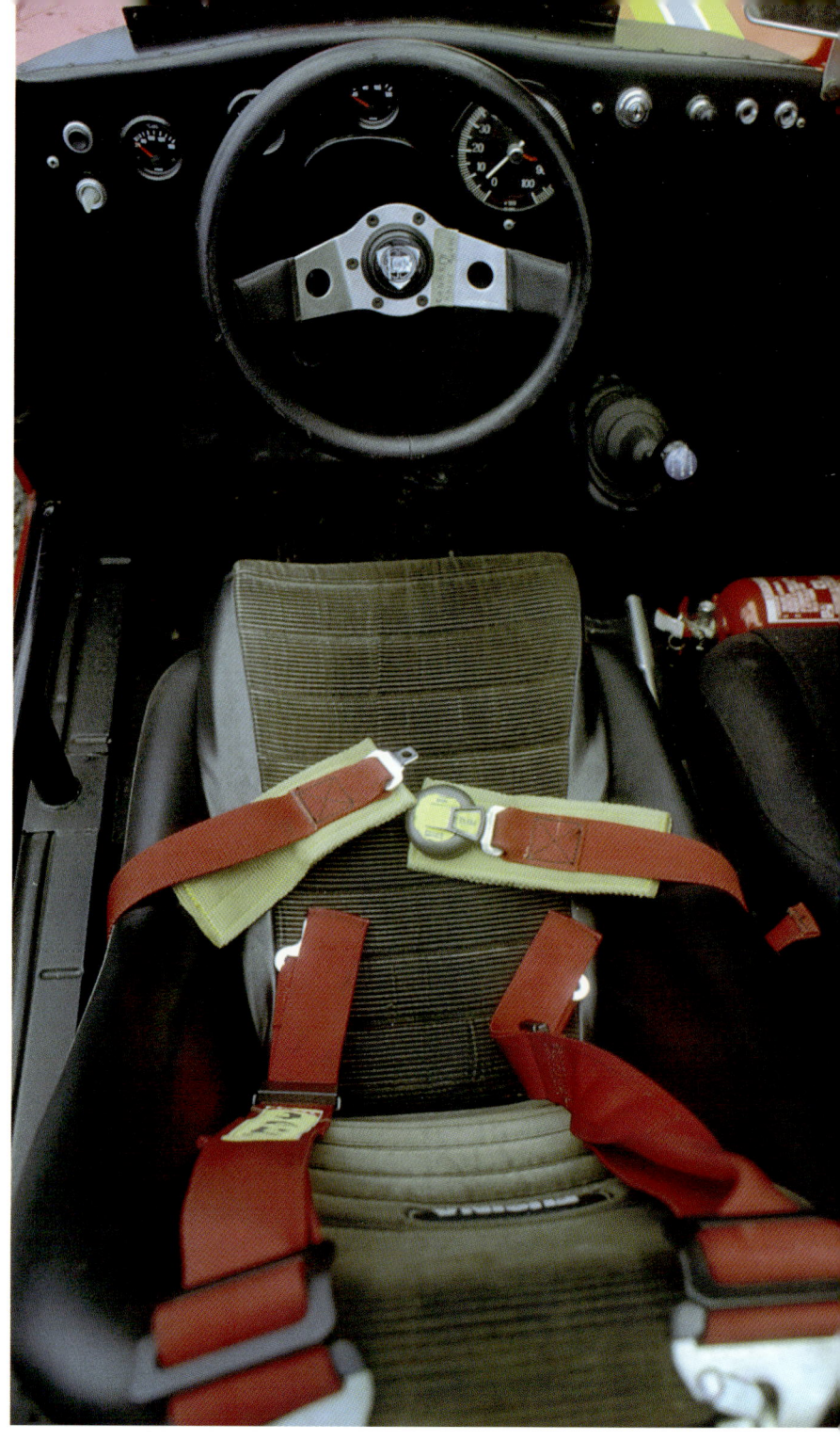

A wrap-around, very anatomic seat in front of a simple aluminium panel boasting four basic dials – a rev counter, oil temperature, pressure and water gauges.

The attractive golden wheel looked very aggressive and the sizeable tyre matched it well.

The characteristic yellow and blue cylinder head of all the racing Fulvias contrasted with four impressive "trumpets" protected by their mesh covers.

The leather-rimmed steering wheel hardly rose above the sides of the car and the minute Plexiglas windscreen did what it could to protect driver and wheel.

This picture of the air intake "trumpets" taken against the light emphasises the fine mesh protection grills while the carburettors take the sun.

155

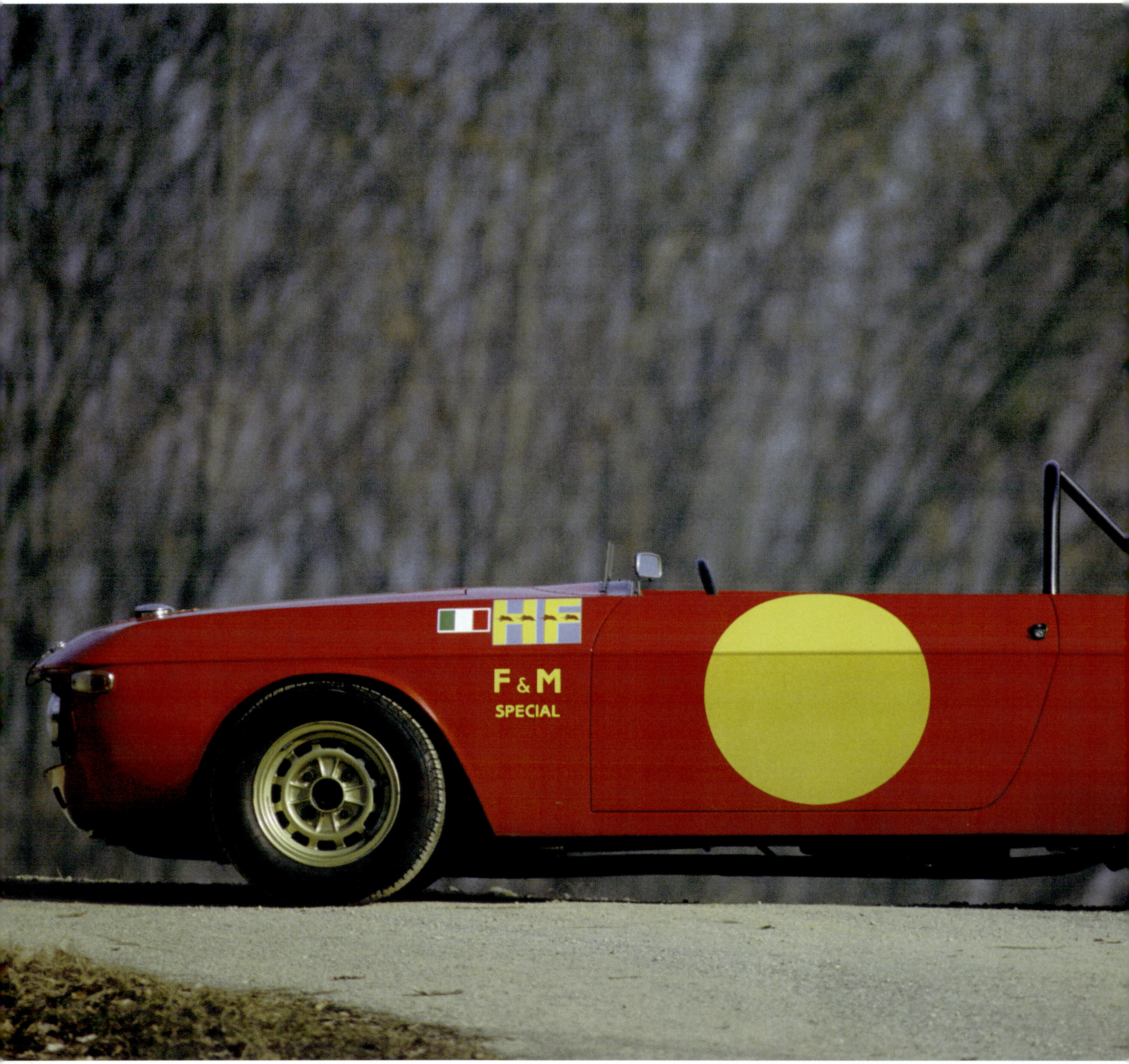
HF
F & M
SPECIAL

Technical specification of the FULVIA F&M SPECIAL

ENGINE: V4 at 11.2°
ENGINE POSITION: front, longitudinal
CUBIC CAPACITY: 1584 cc
BORE AND STROKE: 82x75 mm
DISTRIBUTION: single overhead camshaft per cylinder bank
NUMBER OF VALVES: two per cylinder
COMPRESSION RATIO: 10.5:1
FUEL SUPPLY: two twin choke Solex DDHF carburettors
IGNITION: mono, distributor
COOLING: liquid, front radiator
MAXIMUM POWER: 160 hp at 7800 rpm
MAXIMUM TORQUE: 25 kgm at 5000 rpm
BODY: two-seater open-top in steel, bonnet, boot and doors in aluminium
CHASSIS: load-bearing central monocoq in reinforced sheet metal, with front under-chassis supporting the engine and suspension
SUSPENSION: front – independent, overlapping triangles, telescopic shock absorbers; rear – rigid axle, leaf springs, stabiliser bar
TRANSMISSION: four speed and reverse ZF gearbox, front-wheel drive
CLUTCH: dry mono disc
BRAKES: drums front and rear
DIMENSIONS: length 3907 mm, width 1570 mm, height 840 mm without Plexiglas windscreen
WHEELBASE AND TRACK: front 2330 mm – 1390 mm, rear 1335 mm
TYRES: Michelin XAS 175x13 front and rear
DRY WEIGHT: 720 kg
PERFORMANCE: maximum speed over 140 mph (225 km/h)
ACCELERATION: 0-62 mph (100 km/h) in seven seconds

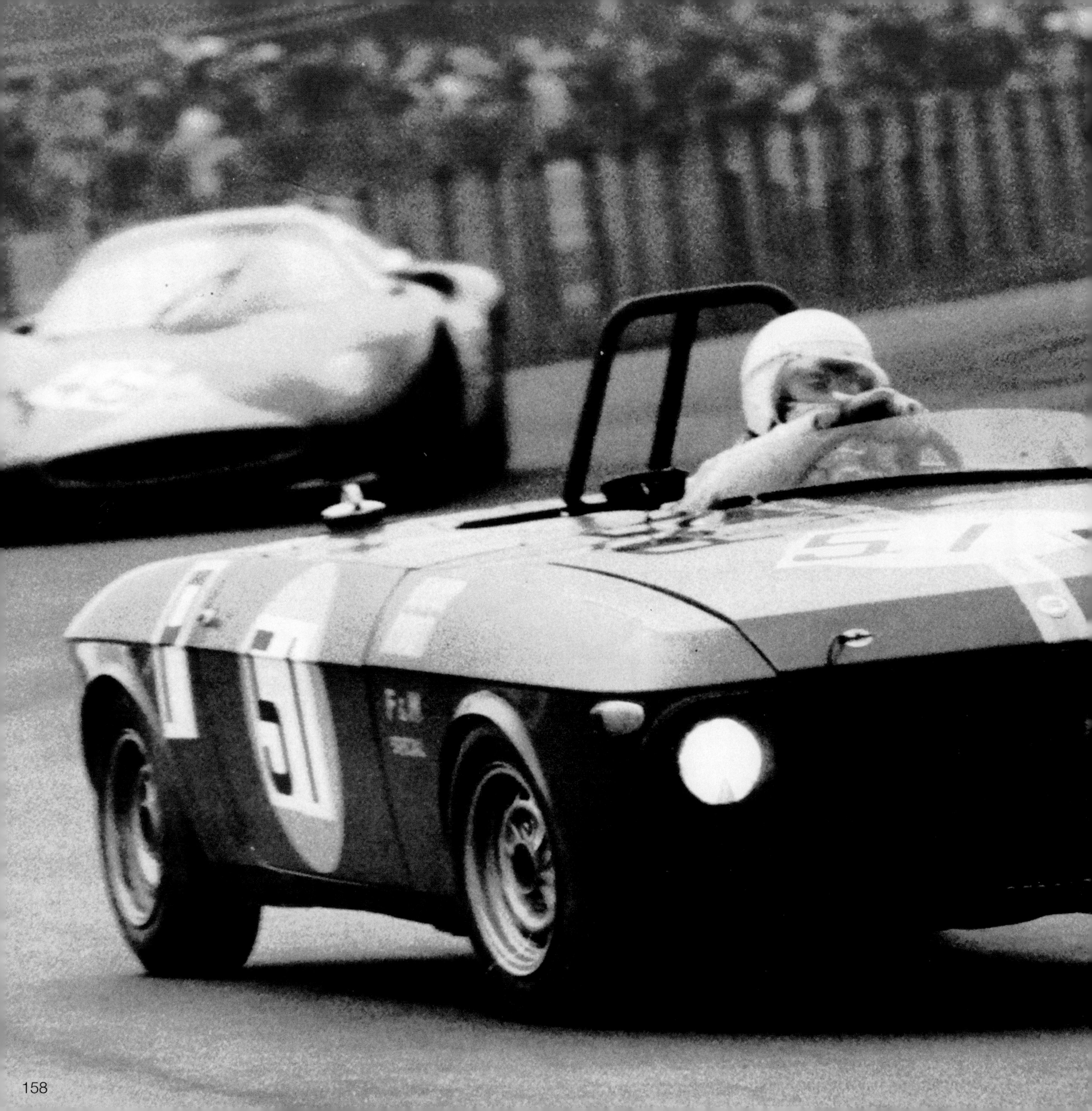

The photographs on pages 158 and 159 appear by courtesy of Claudio Maglioli.

This is the reason why the Maglioli-Pinto F&M Special had to retire from the 1969 Targa Florio: a page of a newspaper blown onto the radiator grill caused the engine to overheat and seize after only three laps.

The Maglioli-Pinto F&M Special in the pits during the 1970 Targa Florio.

Nürburgring, 1969: Claudio Maglioli and his F&M Special barchetta keeping a powerful Lola at bay as it snaps at the little Fulvia's heels.

Tramping down on its offside suspension, the F&M Special shows its race speed: in spite of its limited cubic capacity, the little hybrid could compete successfully against much more powerful cars, even on demanding drivers' circuits like the Nürburgring here in 1969.

159

MONTECARLO

The Lancia Montecarlo won three world endurance championships, the 1979 crown for 2000 cc cars and the overall titles of 1981 and 1982. The car was a fabulous racing coupé that gave Lancia the first of a series of victories since the days of the Stratos some years earlier. A high performance evolution of the Lancia Beta Montecarlo which later gave birth to the 037 rally car, the Montecarlo racer was so full of protrusions and winged surfaces that it almost made observers forget its road car parentage, which could only be seen in the central area of the body. The car's four cylinder in line 1425.9 cc turbocharged engine, which won the 2000 cc class world championship, produced an amazing 480 hp at 9200 rpm in its final form, projecting this missile at over 186 mph (300 km/h). Claudio Maglioli, who prepared the "little" monster with Lancia engineers Tonti and Materazzi, personally developed the engine and said that he increased the power unit's performance in increments, measuring the results as he went. The engine reached an amazing 540 hp and ran for five hours at that level before seizing. Stratospheric performance for a 1400 cc motor, almost comparable to the power of a Formula One engine of the period. And it did not take long for giant-killing Lancia to deliver the results on the track either. This Montecarlo Group 5 car was created at the express wish of Lancia to boost the company's image and sales of the Montecarlo road car, the targa-type coupé that had just been launched. The racer was initially tested with a four cylinder Lancia Gamma boxer engine: but that was only a passing experiment to allow the design team to evaluate the potential and robustness of the would-be racer's chassis and load-bearing central structure, its front and rear sub-frames supporting the engine and suspension. The Gamma 2500 engine, to which a new four valves per cylinder head was fitted, developed a maximum of about 300 hp during this experiment. A supercharged Gamma unit was also tried, but it was not considered ideal for the little Montecarlo. So in the end, the decision was made in favour of the small 1425.9 cc unit. Development work and test driving to bring the engine up to between 460

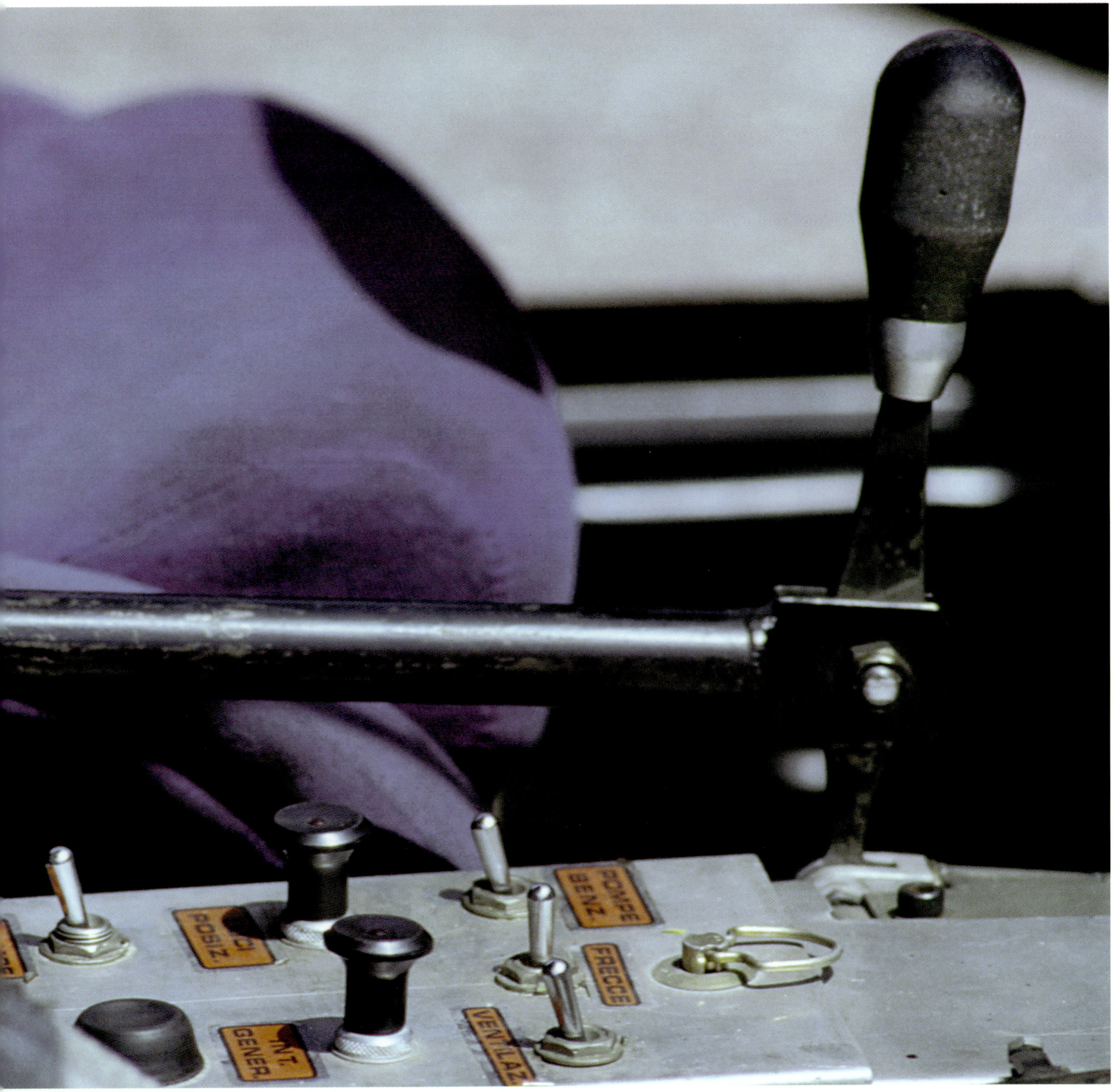
POMPE
BENZ.
FRECCE
POSIZ.
INT.
GENER.
VENTILAZ.

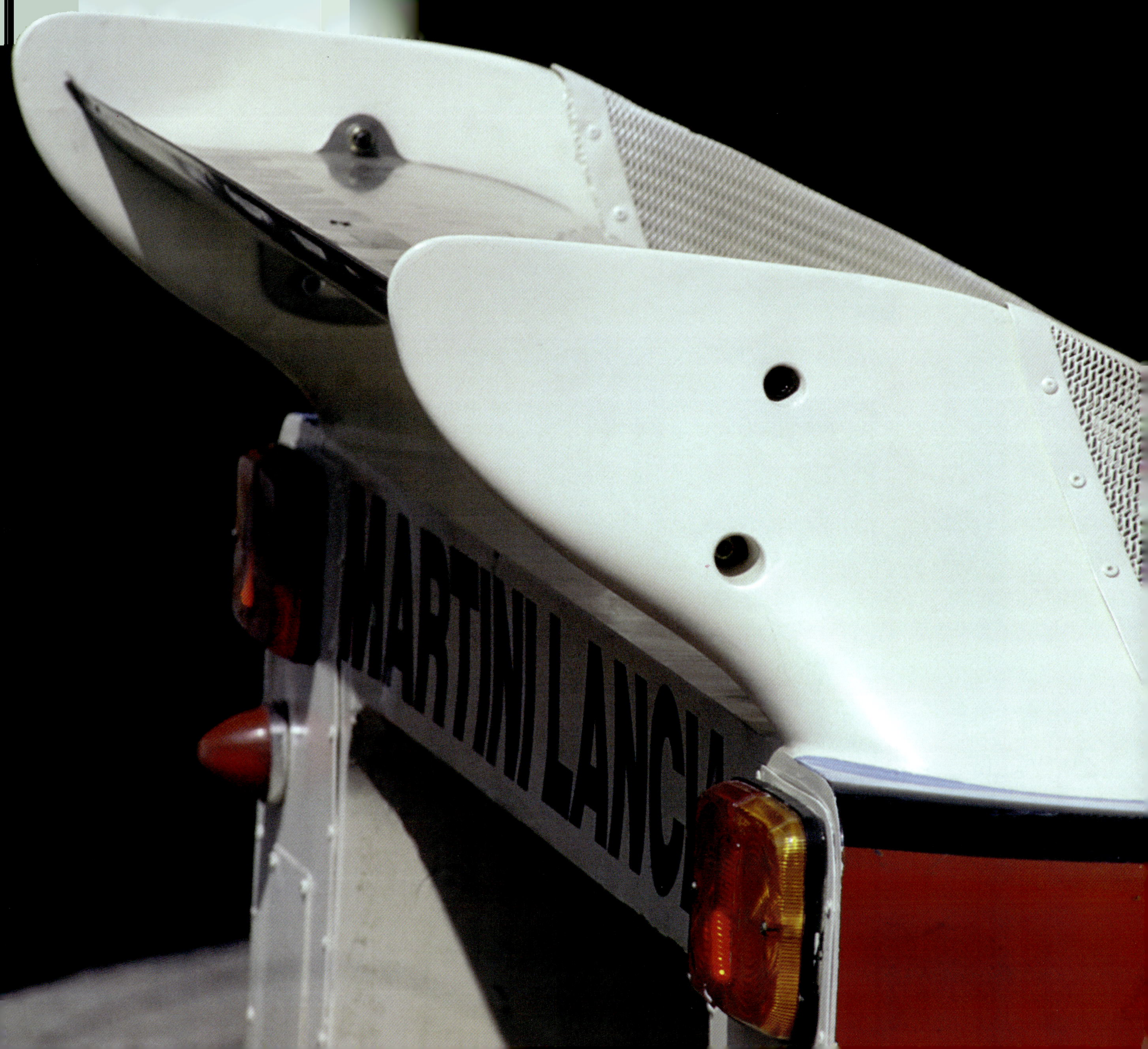
MARTINI LANCIA

hp and 480 hp were carried out in a record time of around three months, so that the car was ready for its first world championship race at Silverstone. With that kind of power at hand, the torque of the small four cylinder was just as phenomenal, producing 55 kg/m at 6500 rpm. All of that power and torque was also attributable to the car's large KKK turbo, a point underlined when opening the lid of the rear engine compartment: the turbo stuck out like the proverbial sore thumb and was the bulkiest component of all. The huge diameter exhausts were no less impressive, jutting out from under the body like two howitzers. For the following season, the engine's cubic capacity was increased to 1429.4 cc and although it gave the car no more power, it did legalise the Montecarlo to compete in the prestigious up to 3000 cc category, which it

The subtle white metal grill elegantly contrasting with the powerful image of the Montecarlo.

A wheel that has been hard at work in a race at Britain's Brands Hatch, with its Pirelli rain tyre.

pininfarina
VS
OLIO
FIAT
sabelt Britax
BILSTEIN
SHOCK ABSORBERS
MAGNETI MARELLI
COLOTTI
TRASMISSIONI
Lubrifilm
MART
PIRELLI P7

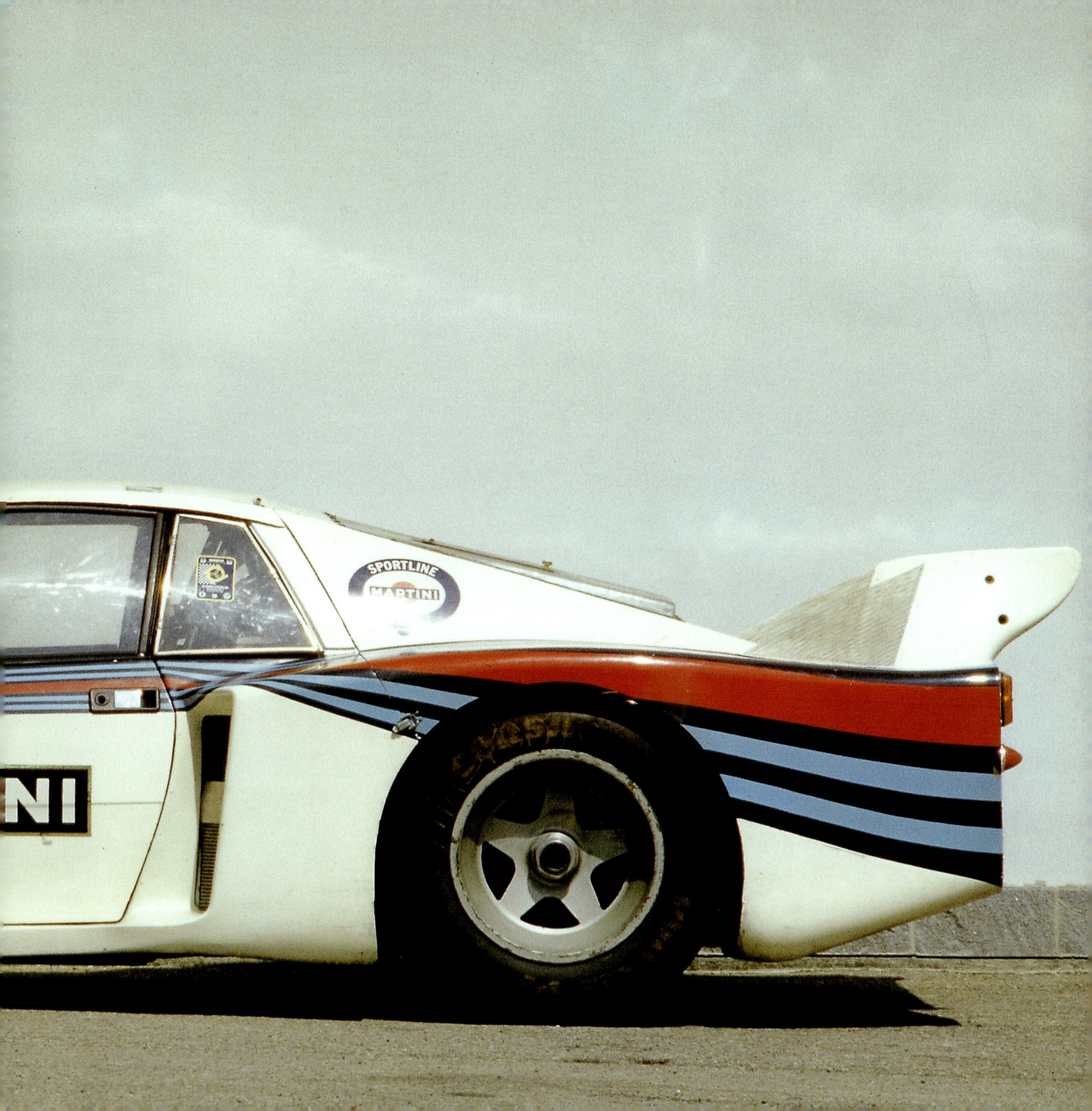
SPORTLINE
MARTINI
NI

MARTINI RACING
MARTINI
pininfarina
sabelt Britax
BILSTEIN
SHOCK ABSORBERS
MAGNETI MARELLI
COLOTTI
TRASMISSIONI
Lubrifilm
VS
OLIO FIAT
PIRELLI
PIRELLI
MARTINI
16

won two years in succession. The final evolution of the engine took its capacity up to 1773 cc and a maximum horsepower increase of about 10 hp, while all other parameters remained more or less the same. A suitable chassis had to be developed to exploit so much power and that delicate task was assigned to Giampaolo Dallara, who sharpened the load-bearing central steel monocoq of the normal production Montecarlo with tubular reinforcement and lightened it with some components in aluminium. To this central section were fitted the front and rear sub-frames, which supported the two ends of the car. A beautiful spider's web of well dimensioned tubes that ensured notable robustness

The Martini livery slightly softened the square lines of the Group 5 Montecarlo, derived from the normal production targa top car. The rear exhaust pipes seem like two large cannons.

and containment of the Montecarlo's weight. The carbon fibre bodyshell was created while being adapted to changes in the dimensions of the car's mechanical components and radiator; in this way, the Montecarlo's appearance matched its performance perfectly. The visual impact of its aggressive shape was a successful example of how to dress a car's mechanics with a skin that also projected a suggestion of the production car's form. Once completed, the Montecarlo

The Fulvia Coupé traffic indicators, flanking a nose unit full of vents and air intakes, travelled a lot faster on this car than the one to which they were originally fitted.

Right: the amply perforated aluminium pedals were able to provide a substantial rush of adrenaline if pushed with the necessary skill.

The big orange indicator in front of the driver was, in a previous life, a Fifties side light.

was taken to the wind tunnel for a number of aerodynamic tests, which meant that the wings on the nose and tail had to be clipped and honed to perfection by the engineers to produce an ideal aerodynamic load and improve road holding at the ultra-high "cruising" speeds of which the car was capable. To handle this thoroughbred, Lancia engaged some of the leading drivers of the day, all of them from Formula One and other high level disciplines of motor sport. They included Michele Alboreto, Eddie Cheever, Andrea De Cesaris, Beppe Gabbiani, Piercarlo Ghinzani and Hans Heyer. Even some of the top rally drivers turned their hand to Group 5 and drove the Montecarlo, including Walter Rohrl, who gave the car its first competitive outing at Silverstone and the late Gilles Villeneuve in the 79th Giro d'Italia, both with Riccardo Patrese. A subsequent edition of the Giro was actually won by drivers from the two worlds of track racing and rallying: Riccardo Patrese and Markku Alen's co-driver Illka Kivimaki came first and Michele Alboreto with the late Atillio Bettega second. The career of the Montecarlo was a short one in spite of the outstanding results it achieved: Lancia was already thinking of an "ultimate weapon" with which to compete for the World Endurance Championship. The design and development of the new car absorbed a great deal of energy, which was eventually rewarded with concrete results. But it was the Montecarlo that opened the road to success in the best possible way; next, though it was the LC2's turn.

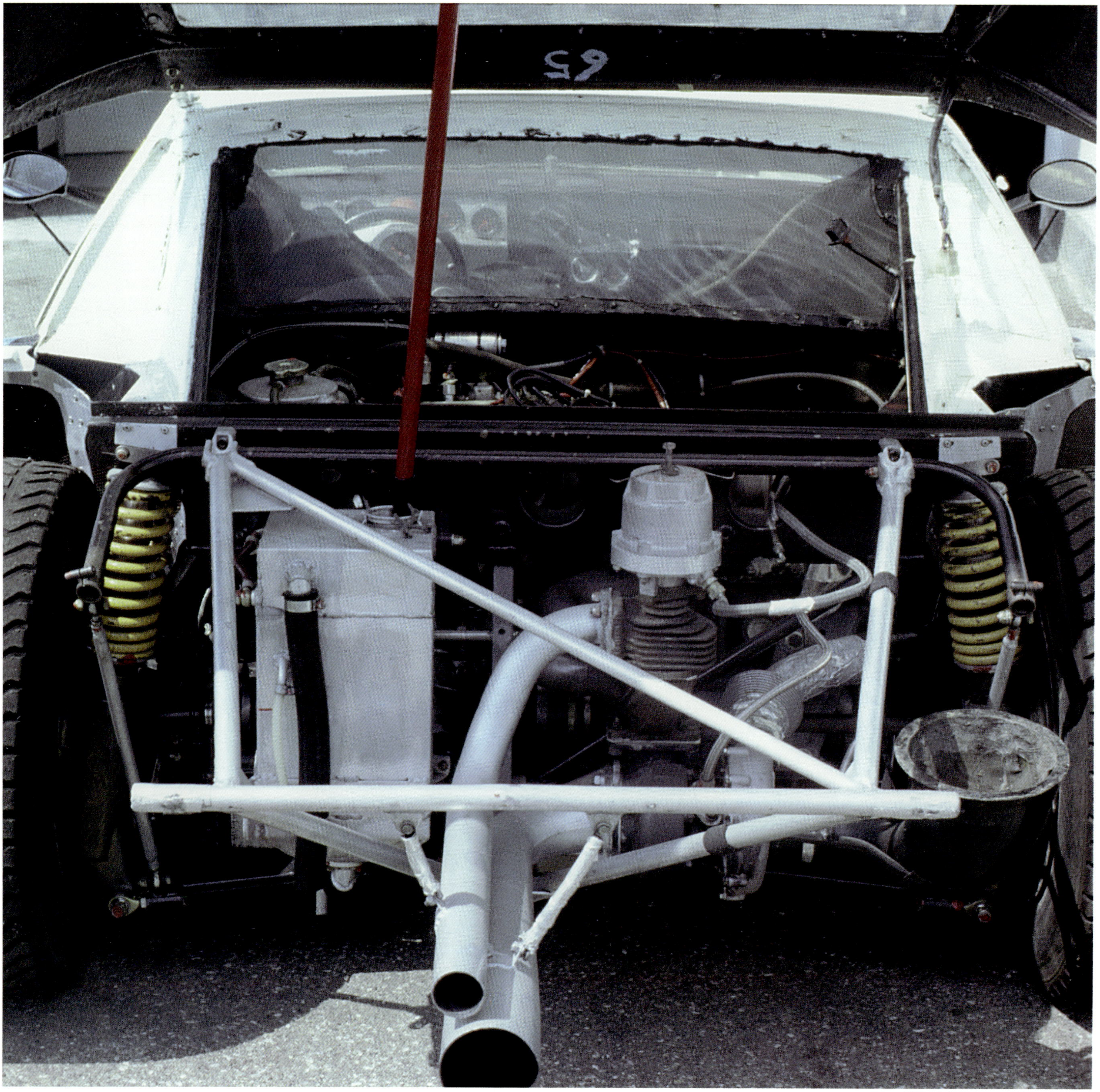

Opposite page: a virtual striptease reveals the Montecarlo's large fuel tank, mounted in the front to even out the weight of the car.

When opening the rear hood of the Montecarlo its compact powerplant looked impressive.

171

Technical specifications of the MONTECARLO

ENGINE: four cylinders in line
ENGINE POSITION: rear, longitudinal
CUBIC CAPACITY: 1425.9 cc (cat. version 3000 1429.4 cc)
BORE AND STROKE: 82x67.5 mm (cat. 3000 82.1 x 67.5 mm)
DISTRIBUTION: twin belt-driven overhead camshafts
NUMBER OF VALVES: four per cylinder
COMPRESSION RATIO: 6.5:1
FUEL SUPPLY: Weber-Marelli I.A.W. electronic injection, KKK turbo
IGNITION: Weber-Marelli I.A.W. electronic
LUBRIFICATION: dry sump
COOLING: liquid, one front radiator
MAXIMUM POWER: 400/450 hp at 9000/9500 rpm
MAXIMUM TORQUE: 36,5 kg/m at 6500 rpm
BODY: two-seater coupé, body shell in resin and composite
CHASSIS: central load-bearing monocoq in steel
SUSPENSION: independent all round, front stabiliser bar, double rear shock absorbers
TRANSMISSION: five speed and reverse gearbox; self-locking differential
CLUTCH: dry bi-disc
BRAKES: self-ventilating, perforated discs all round
DIMENSIONS: length 4600 mm, width 1990 mm, height 1100 mm
WHEELBASE AND TRACK: front 2300 mm – 1440 mm, rear 1570 mm
TYRES: front: 16x10,5 (1978); 15x10 (1980); 16x11,5 (1981)
rear: 16x13,5 (1978); 19x13,5 (1980); 19x14,5 (1981)
DRY WEIGHT: 780 kg
PERFORMANCE: maximum speed over 186 mph (300 km/h), depending on the gear ratios

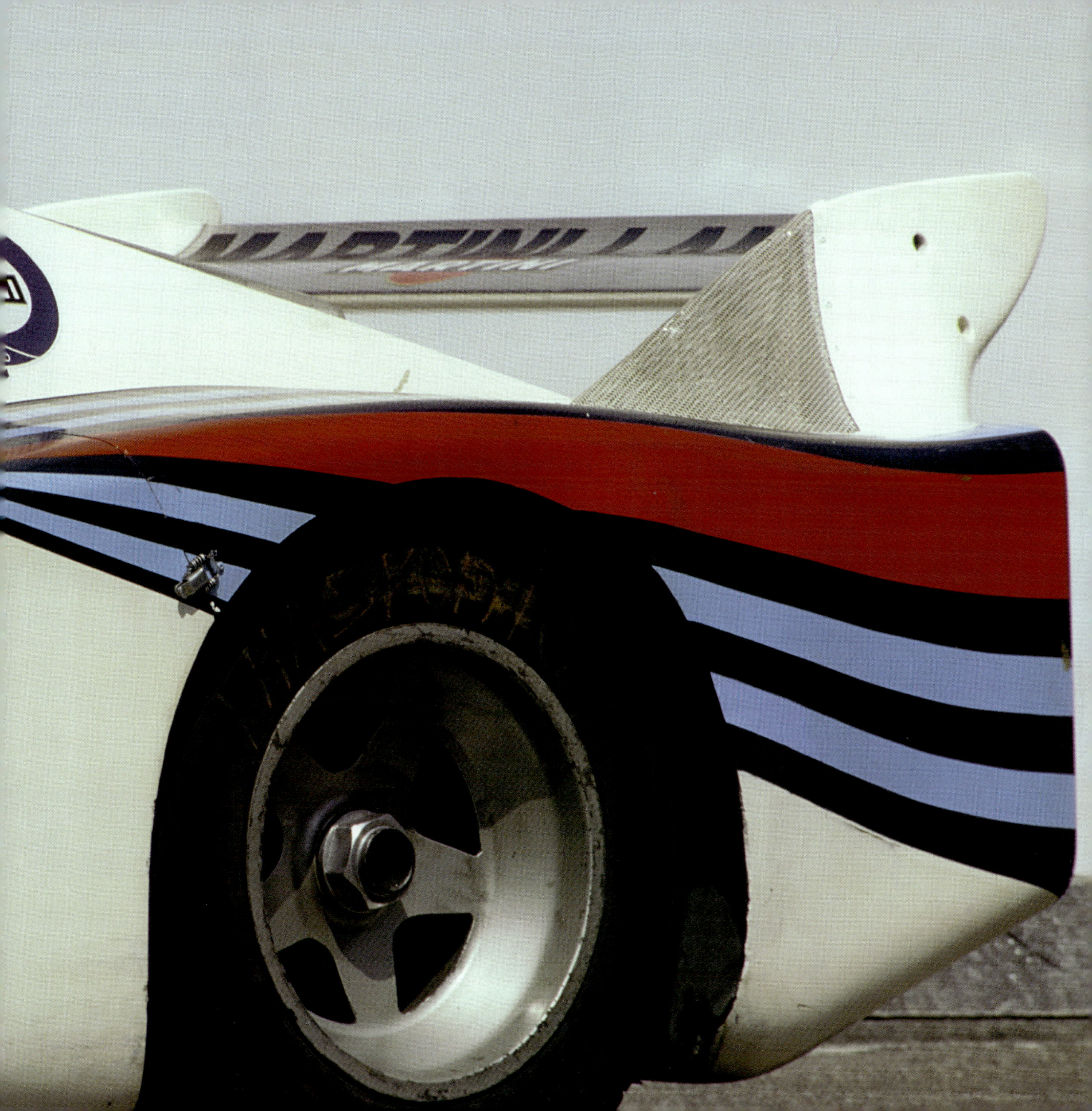
MARTINI

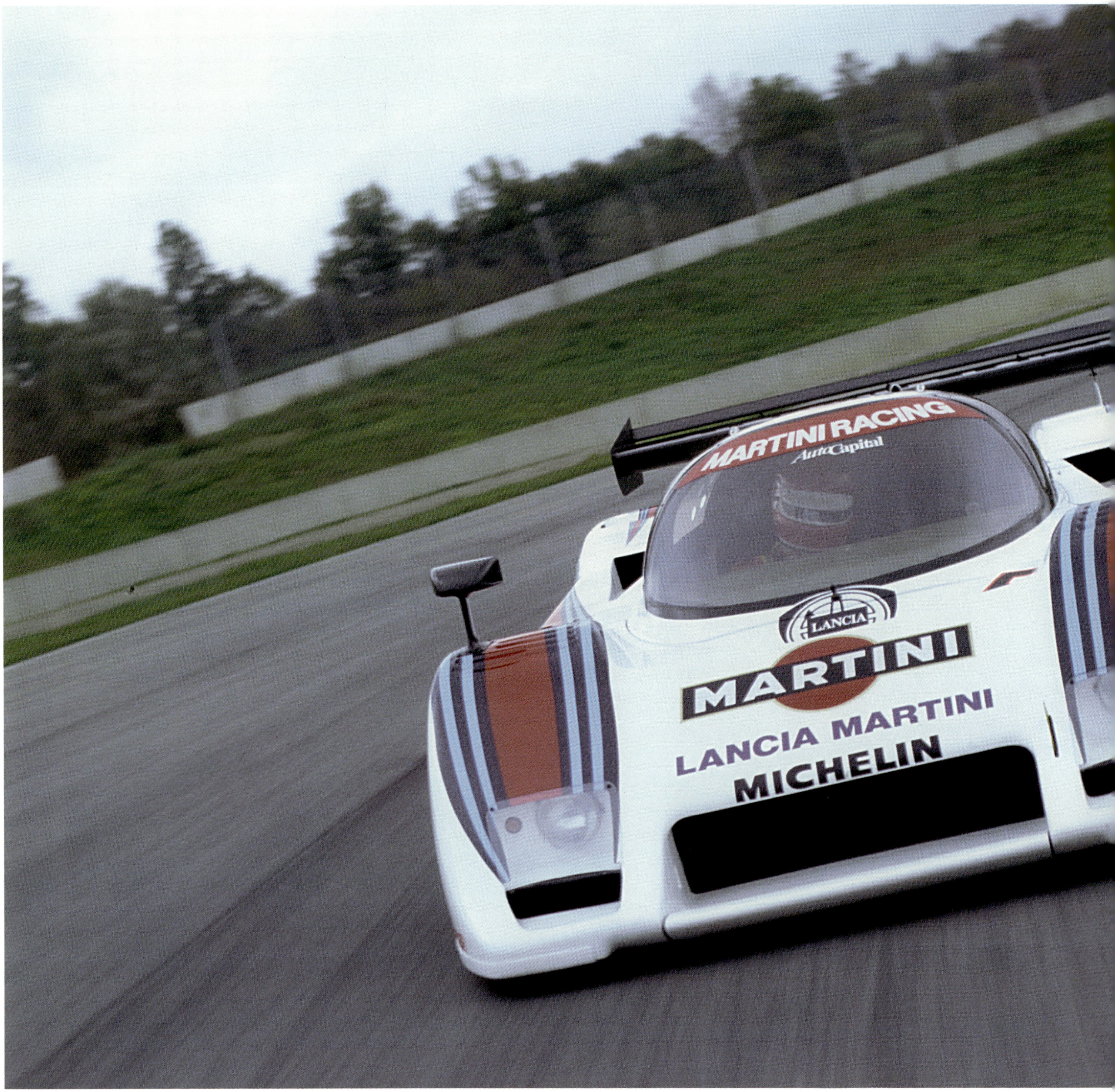

LC2

Lancia and Ferrari, a union with roots reaching deep down into the history of motor racing. One that harks back to the D 50, which was so important to the development of the Turin manufacturer in competition and six of which were ceded to Ferrari, only to win the 1956 Formula One World Championship in the hands of Juan Manuel Fangio. The LC2 project first got off the ground in 1982 after the Group 5 open top LC1 had signalled the official return of Lancia to track racing. Once again, chassis design became the responsibility of Giampaolo Dallara, one of whose early successes was the Lamborghini Miura and who developed the LC2 package in his "factory" at Vairano. Time was short because Lancia wanted to debut the car at the 1000 Kilometres of Monza, but they made it. On 9 February, 1983, the first LC2 prototype was shown to the press and soon afterwards this magnificent-looking track racer was ready to face the highly competitive gang of Porsche 956s which, up until then, ruled as the unchallenged dominator of this form of motor racing. Two cars were entered for Monza, one driven by Piercarlo Ghinzani and Teo Fabi, the other by Michele Alboreto and Riccardo Patrese. As far as top performance was concerned, the debut was promising: the Ghinzani-Fabi car took pole but unfortunately it did not see the chequered flag, meanwhile the Alboreto-Patrese car came ninth. This first series used a 2600 cc engine that was replaced in 1984 by a higher performance 3000 cc unit. During the 1983 season the LC2 experienced many mechanical reliability problems, even though its performance showed it was a match for the competition, if not superior to it. The car competed in 9 of the championship's races, winning at Imola, coming second at Mugello and Kyalami and lower down the field in other events: even so, at the end of the season the Lancia came second in the World Championship for Manufacturers. For 1984, the company's head of motor sport, Cesare Fiorio, added Mauro Baldi, Alessandro Nannini and Bob Wolleck to his team of drivers. The new season brought some improvement as far as the car's reliability was concerned, but tyre problems, which the team had already experienced during the preceding season, often meant the LC2 did not finish. Even so, the car did achieve some useful results, notably victories at Spa-Francorchamps and in

175

Japan. The reliability problems of the LC2, which occurred with worrying regularity, were mainly caused by the fragility of a number of mechanical components, like rear half-shafts which were under severe stress from the massive power of the engine, and sometimes by the extremely sophisticated electronic management system that controlled the engine's operation. But 1985 was not a major race-winning year for the Lancia. The works LC2s retired from racing (there were also two privately entered cars belonging to Scuderia Mirabella and the newly formed Team Mussato Action Car) on the eve of the Nuremberg race, partly because one of the car's test drivers had been killed trying out an LC2 on Fiat's La Mandrill track. Deep distress at the loss contributed to the retirement of Lancia from the race and, unfortunately, from the World Endurance Championship. The LC2, however, was not pensioned off. The works cars were bought by Gianni Mussato and they returned to racing under the banner of his team; subjected to continual evolution, the Mussato LC2s competed in the World Endurance championship for a number of years, driven by men of the calibre of Andrea De Cesaris and Bruno Giacomelli. Long tailed versions of the Team Mussato LC2s competed in the mythical 24 Hours of Le Mans four times, a set up which was also used at Silverstone. But then the ups and downs of the Endurance Championship and the consequent loss of

Positioned low along the side of the LC2 were the two dominant exhausts and the rear view mirror, which jutted up almost as high as the car's roof.

The LC2 with its doors and rear engine compartment open, a configuration of outstanding beauty, which amazed all who saw it.

MARTINI RACING
MARTINI RACING
MARTINI
LANCIA MARTINI
MICHELIN
WEBER
WEBER
FERODO

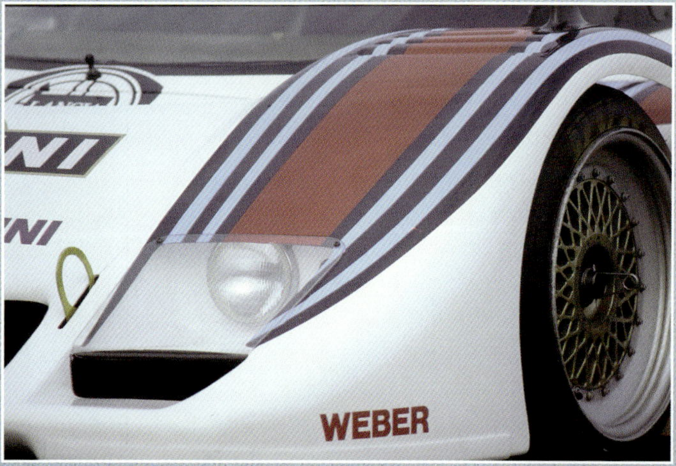
WEBER

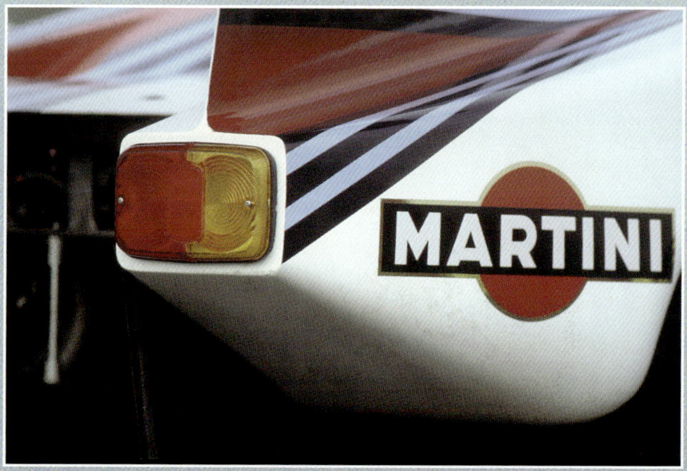
MARTINI

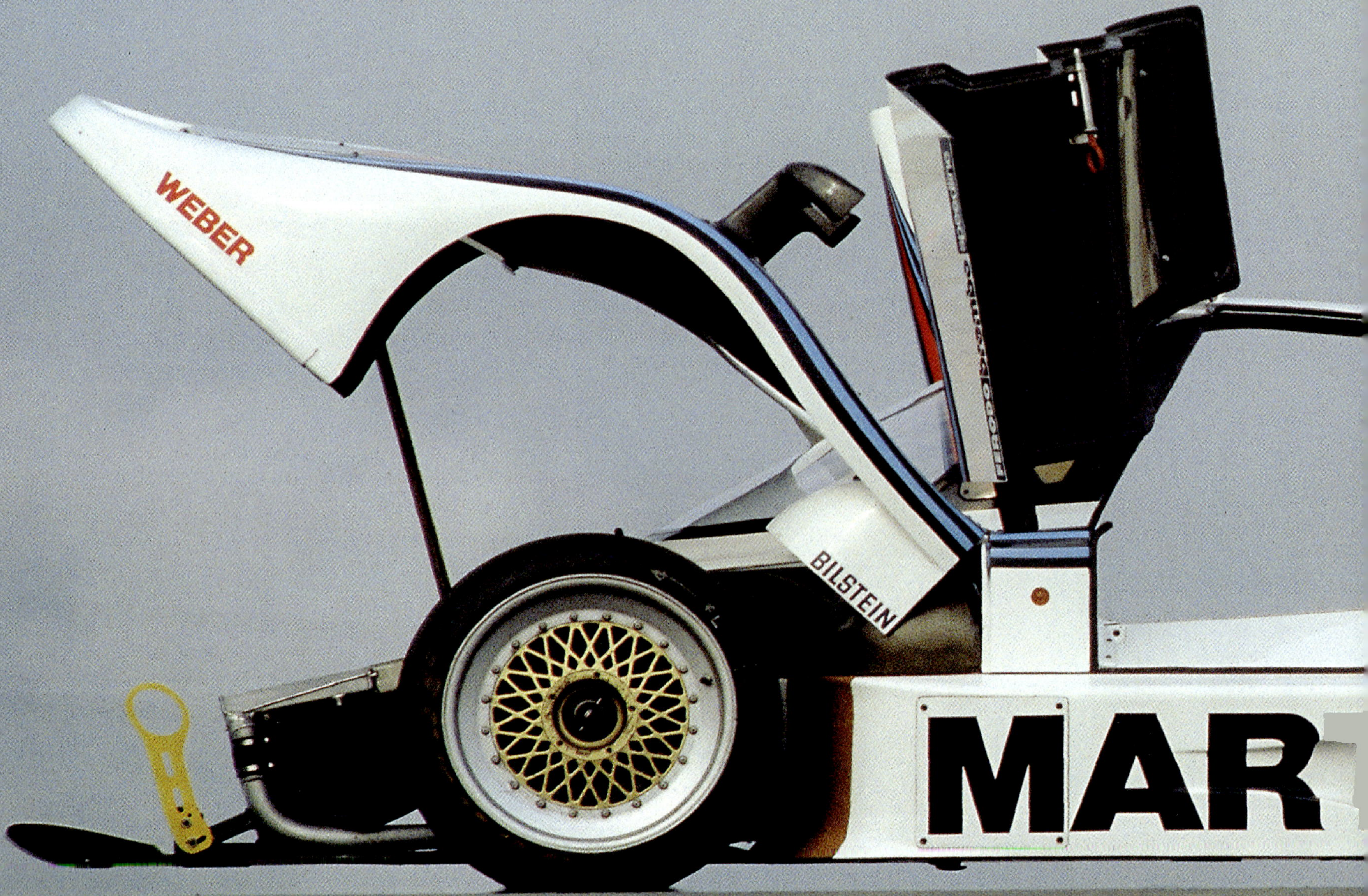
WEBER
BILSTEIN

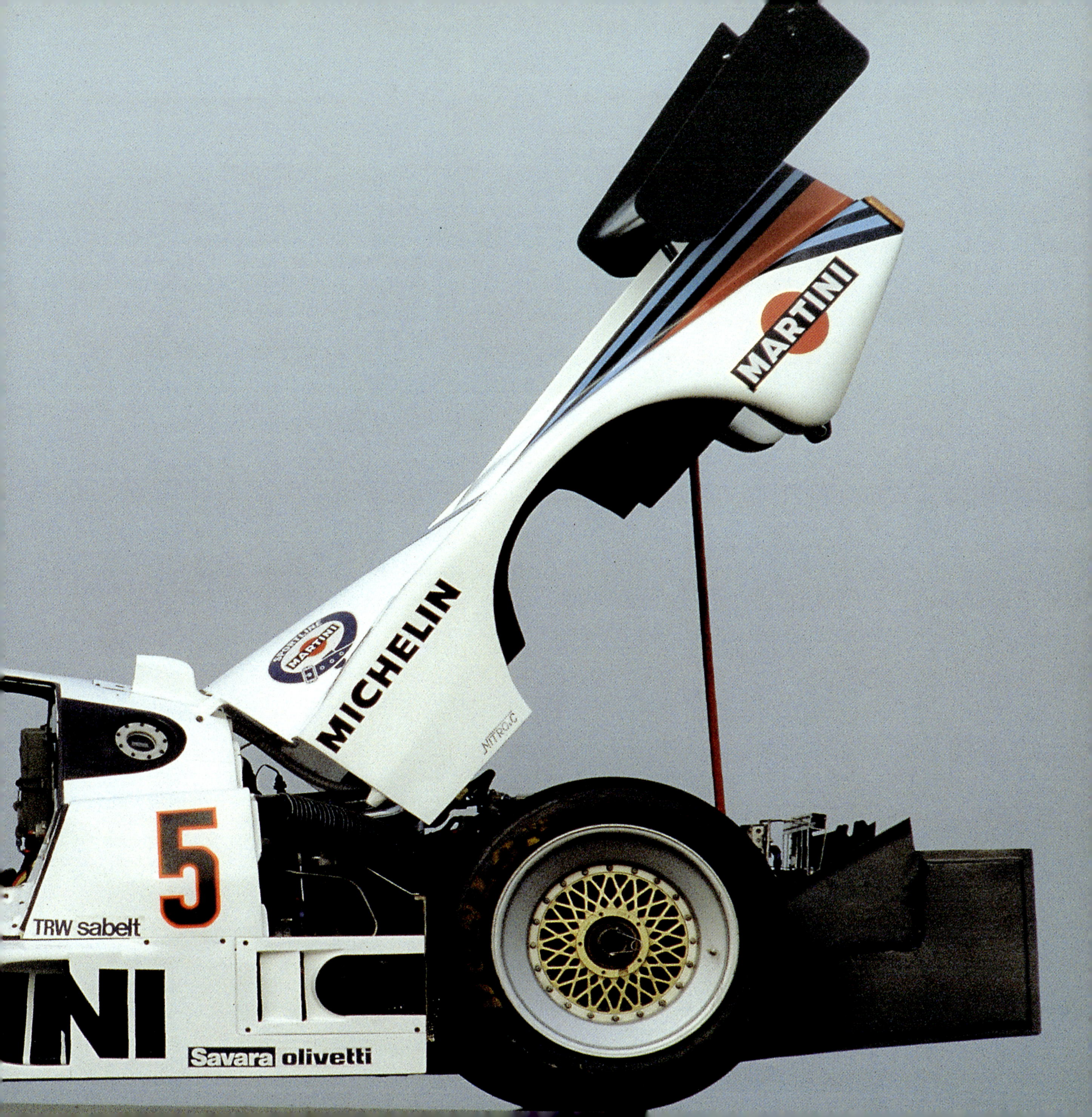
MARTINI
MICHELIN
5
TRW sabelt
Savara olivetti

the sponsor interest for this kind of racing, led to the definitive retirement of the LC2 in 1991 after eight years of honourable battle on the racetracks of the world. To be precise, Mussato built 11 examples of the car, some of which were written off in racing. The Lancia pictured in this chapter is in sprint configuration and includes the short tail used in the 1000 Kms of Monza; this car took about a year to assemble in the workshop of a well-known Maranello mechanic. The chassis, the last of its kind produced by the Lancia racing department but which was never raced, hosted an extremely powerful Ferrari V8 engine and all was beautifully shrouded in a sleek carbon fibre skin painted in Martini colours by Nitro C, the same company that liveried the car when it was racing. With a weight of about 850 kg and a power output of 840 hp (imagine the power-to-weight ratio!) this great "roller skate" was able to power itself to a minimum of 211 mph (340 km/h) and a maximum of 242 mph (390 km/h), depending on the gear ratios, rocketing from 0-62 mph in far less than three seconds. Producing a V8 twin-turbo engine like this was a true feat of electronic engineering: only a purpose-built on-board computer was able to inject exactly the right dosage of air/fuel and transmit data to the sophisticated Weber-Marelli engine management system of this LC2 to make the eight Mahle metal pistons pulsate so that they returned precisely 9000 beats a minute. The car's Ferrari engine was fitted with a 288 GTO cylinder head, but treated at extremely high temperature to guarantee greater hardness of the aluminium alloy. On the other hand, the crankcase was purpose-designed and built and was of the dry sump type. The two KKK turbines, fitted with Behr intercoolers, had big diameter 67 mm rotors – 72 mm were used for the faster circuits - and were able to work at a maximum pressure of three bar. They came into operation in pairs at around 3000 rpm. As far as torque goes, try to imagine how many kilograms per metre this monster of an engine produced at less than 5000 rpm (4800 rpm to be precise). The answer is a frightening 111 kg/m: like a motor torpedo boat! As well as being a mechanical jewel, this very sophisticated engine, coded the 271 L, was also an aesthetic masterpiece with its shiny inlet manifolds in Dural welded by TIG, the Aerokip tubing for fuel and oil and the Elektron gearbox, which lies maliciously in the rear of the bodyshell, flashing at those who followed it. And what is there to say about the turbines and their exhaust manifolds with their relative terminals made in Inconal, the sophisticated material also used for the afterburners of Tornado jet fighters: it is better to not even think about the temperatures they were able to withstand! The only "human" parts of this extra-terrestrial creature were the rear lights, which came from a Fiat 238 van: they travelled a little faster on the rear end of the LC2! Braking the Lancia Competizione 2 was the responsibility of four enormous long player-size, 13.4-inch discs

Wedged-shaped, close to the ground, the LC2's nose in profile immediately manifests the car's aggressive spirit.

A wing appendage of large proportions guaranteed the composure of the LC2's rear end at speed.

The only possible view a terrestrial vehicle could have of this earth-to-earth missile, which allows malicious intuition to only guess at what is in the rear engine compartment, with all those aluminium shapes dressing its powerful spirit.

which were, naturally, perforated, self-ventilating and with four-piston callipers that were equally large. Under the front and rear hoods, carbon fibre coexisted with expensive alloys: the rear aerodynamic extractors, the flat rear end and the front structure to which the nose was fixed were in fact of such material. The chassis was in Avional (a special aluminium alloy) panelled onto ribs of magnesium with wind braces in titanium. In the single seat interior, there was Avional almost everywhere, with a few exceptions including the driver's seat and the upper cover of the instrument panel, both of which were in carbon fibre. It was almost a case of the driver being "dressed" in this superb Group C Lancia. Once he had lowered himself into the car, remaining space permitted little further movement than the essential: operating the pedals, manoeuvring the gear lever and imposing the trajectory of the car with the steering wheel. But what else was there to do inside such a beast? Seated less than four inches above the ground (the flat bottom was 7 cms above the asphalt) faced by a circular instrument with its red line at 9000 rpm, a series of dials and switches

Designed by the wind, the body of the LC2 has a sophisticated skin of costly fibre covering its muscles.

181

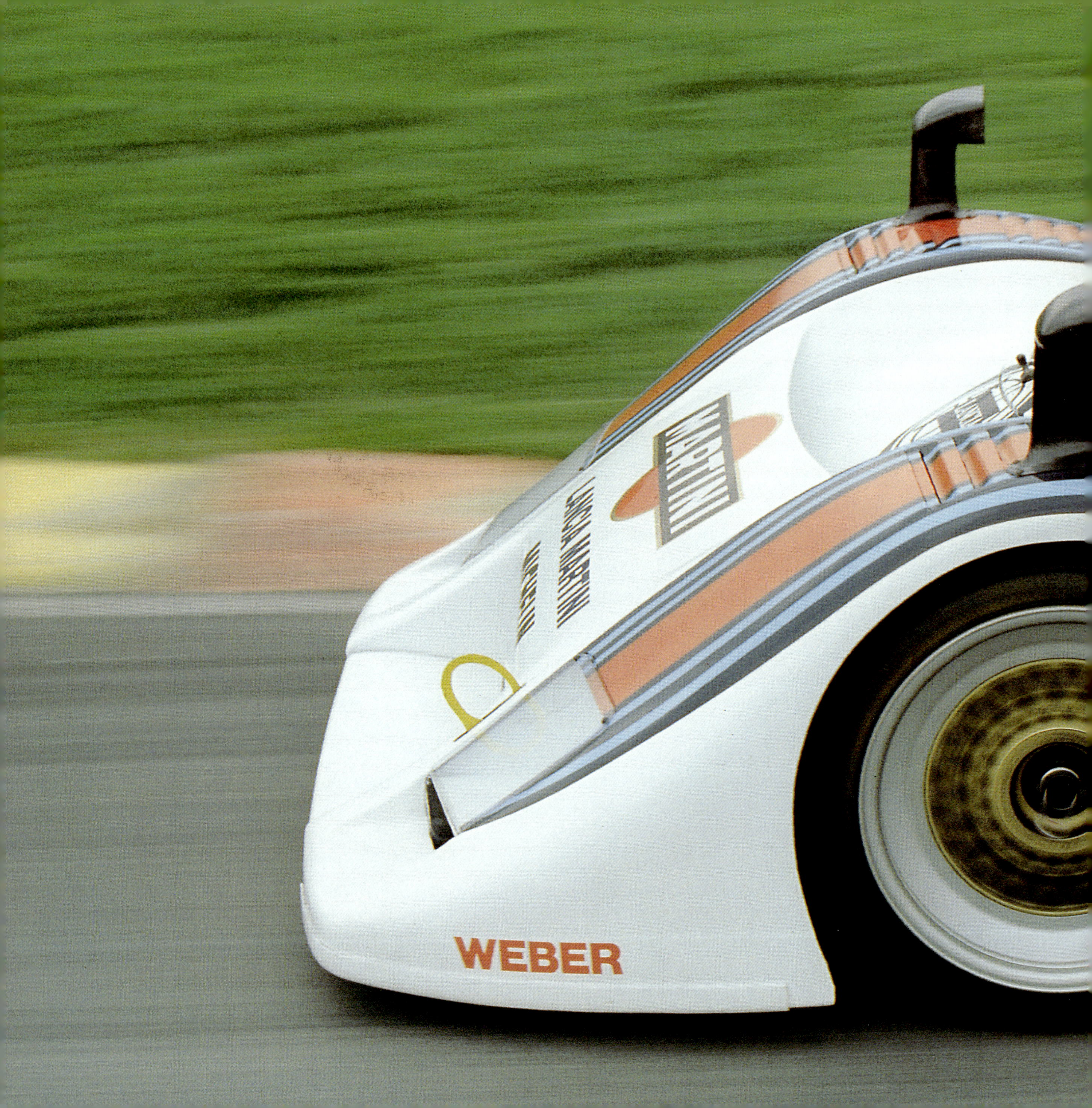
WEBER

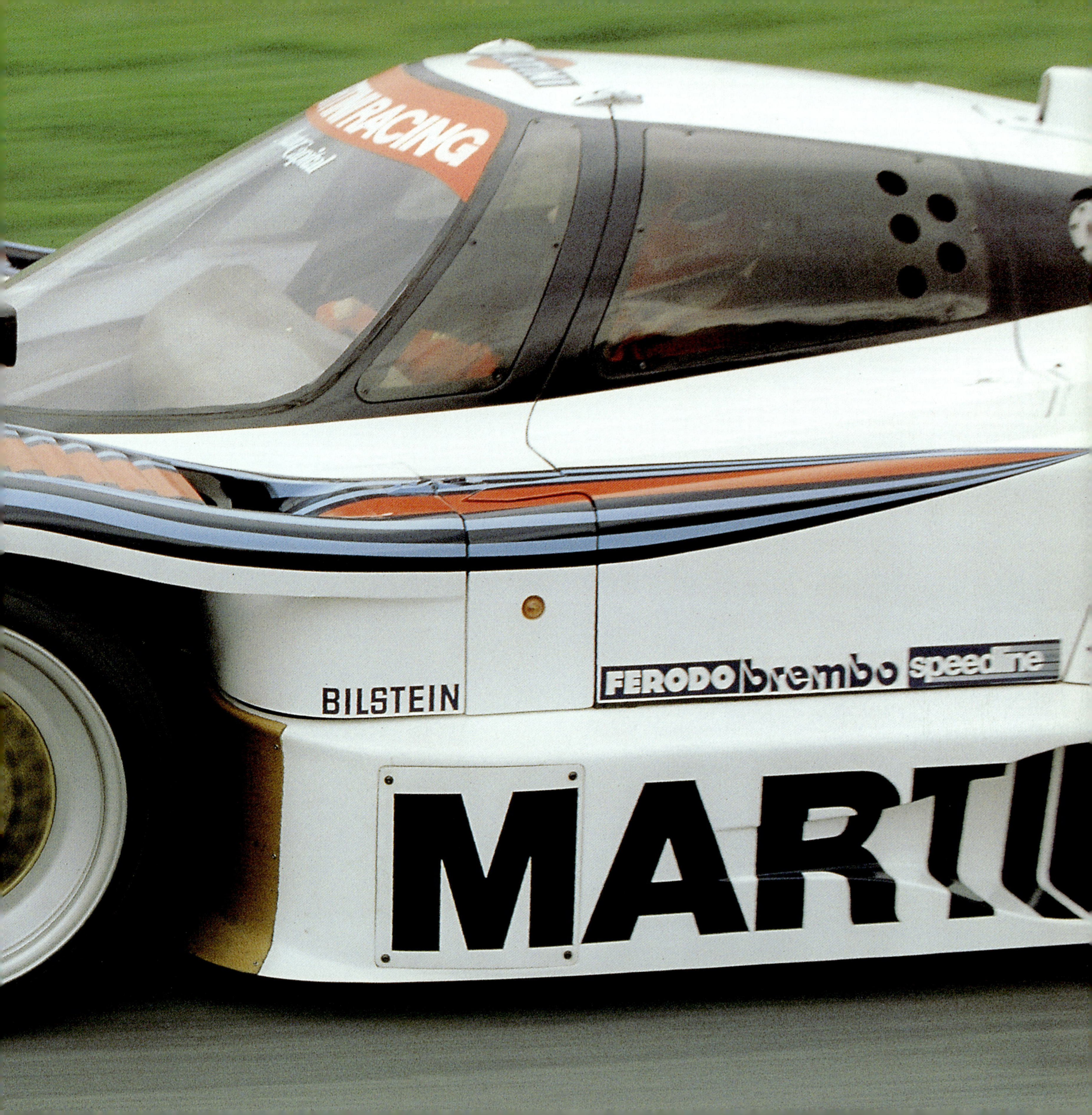
BILSTEIN
FERODO
brembo
speedline

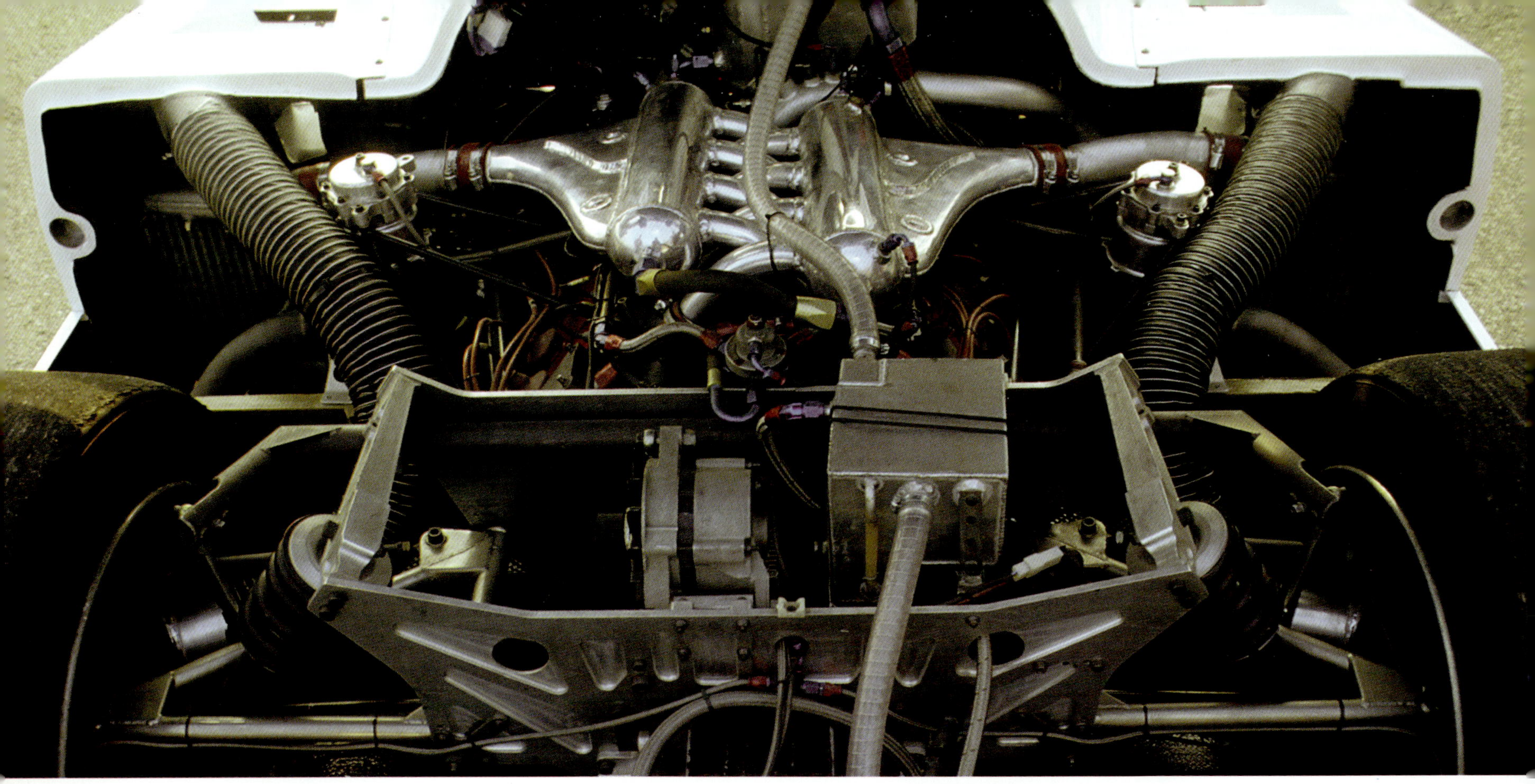

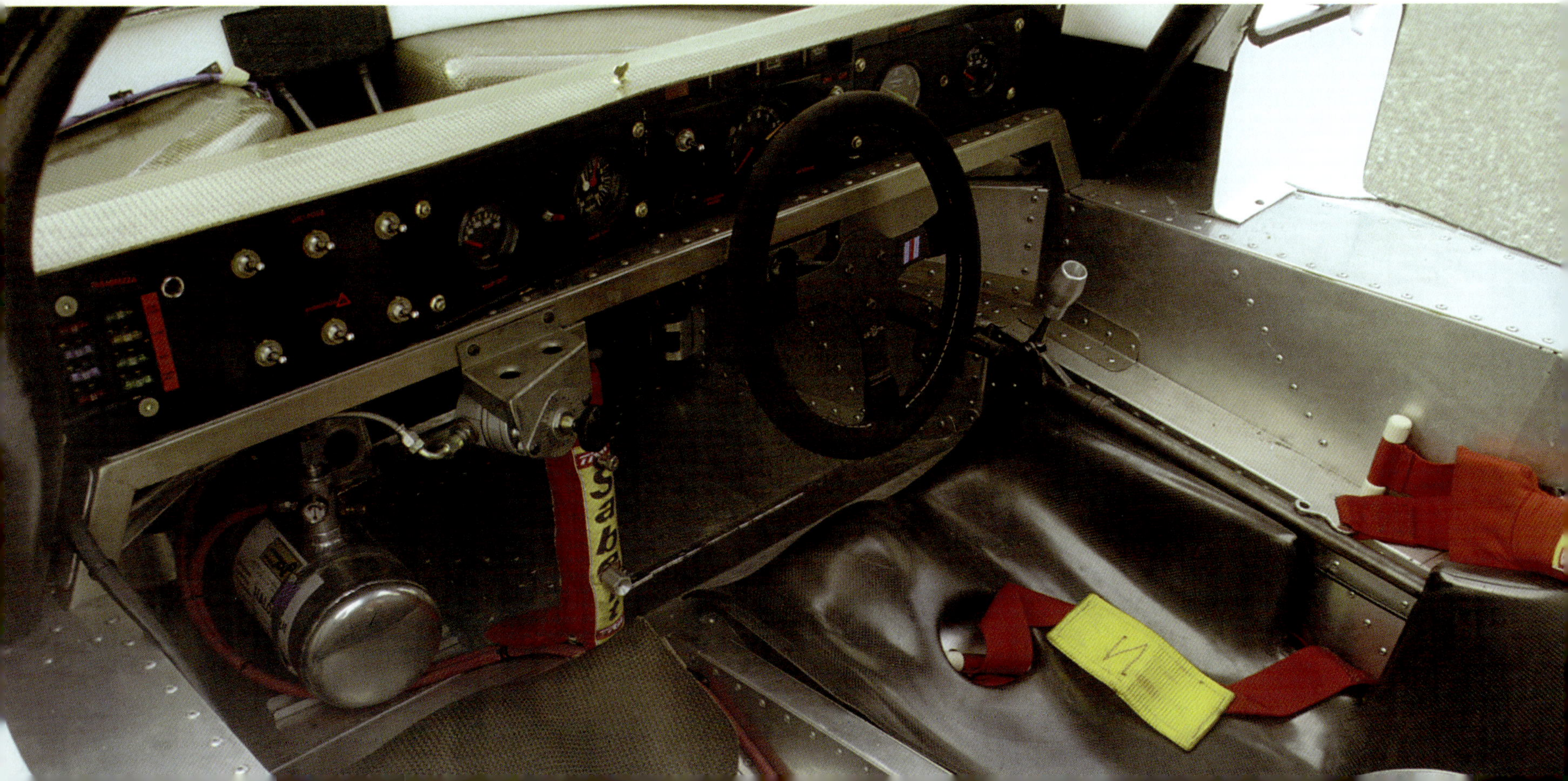

In the vastness of the engine compartment, aluminium is the boss: an 840 hp power output deserves refined technology and aesthetics.

Almost all the technology that comprised the LC2 was Italian: the attractive front radiator comes from the same city as the car itself, Turin.

The sleek TIG welding work which "decorates" the extremely shiny exhaust manifold is just one of the car's many technological refinements.

The small, chamois-rimmed steering wheel is an extremely direct means of communication between this supercar and mother Earth.

The pressure gauge of the turbine, calibrated up to four atmospheres, gives an immediate idea of the power of the LC2.

Left: Not so dissimilar to that of a jet fighter, the narrow cockpit of the LC2 must be "worn" tightly to savour the powerful emotions the car can guarantee.

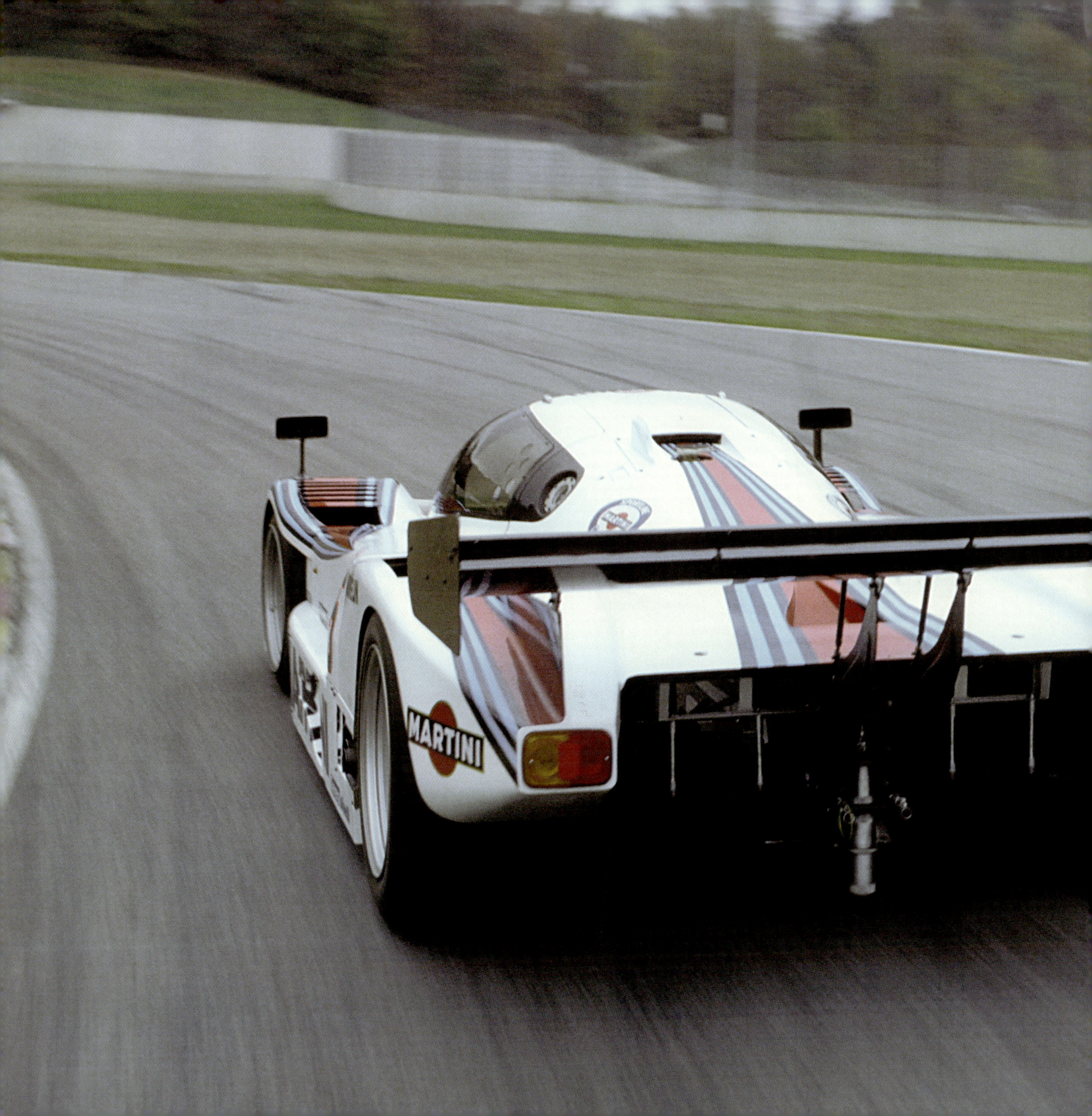
MARTINI

Technical specification of the LC2

ENGINE: V8 at 90°
ENGINE POSITION: rear centre, longitudinal
CUBIC CAPACITY: 2999 cc
BORE AND STROKE: 84x70 mm
DISTRIBUTION: twin overhead camshafts per cylinder bank
NUMBER OF VALVES: four per cylinder
COMPRESSION RATIO: 7.5:1
FUEL SYSTEM: Weber-Marelli indirect electronic injection, two KKK turbos
IGNITION: Weber-Marelli I.A.M. indirect electronic
COOLING: forced circulation liquid, one front radiator
MAXIMUM POWER: 840 hp at 7000 rpm
MAXIMUM TORQUE: 111 kg/m at 5500 rpm
BODY: single-seater coupé, composite body
CHASSIS: Avional with central monocoq in carbon fibre
SUSPENSION: independent front and rear, four-sided transversal arms, double helicoidal springs
TRANSMISSION: rear-wheel drive, Hewland gearbox with five forward gears and a reverse, rigid rear axle
CLUTCH: Borg and Beck bi-disc
BRAKES: self-ventilating perforated discs front and rear
DIMENSIONS: (short sprint version) length 4850 mm, width 2000 mm, height 1040 mm
WHEELBASE AND TRACK: front 2680 mm – 1550 mm, rear 1600 mm
TYRES: front 275-17, rear 350-19
DRY WEIGHT: 850 kg
PERFORMANCE: maximum speed from 211 mph (340 km/h) to 242 mph (390 km/h) depending on gear ratios and aerodynamic configuration
ACCELERATION: 0-62 mph (100 km/h) in 2.4 seconds

Scenes from the 1984 1000 Kilometres of Monza, with Piercarlo Ghinzani and Riccardo Patrese in the pits and at that fatal moment when a tyre blew.

to make an F16 envious, a lever to the right surmounted by a small aluminium knob, the only thing that could come spontaneously would be to stamp on the right pedal and feel the effect that has. But it is better to hear what it is like to drive this powerful beast from someone who really knows how and who has driven it many times on the circuits of the world: we asked Bruno Giacomelli to talk us through a lap of Monza at the wheel of an LC2. "After a warm-up lap, I shoot along the straight past the pits in fifth to arrive at the approach to the Goodyear chicane at 222 mph (358 km/h), according to the photo-electric cells, at 8500 rpm. I stamp on the brakes at the 200-metre marker and drop down three gears to take the first left-hander of the Goodyear in second. To compensate for the understeer caused by the blocked differential, I clip the red and white hard shoulder with my right wheel to create a little oversteer to help me impose the right trajectory, a trick which is often used with cars whose rear wheels rotate at the same speed". Child's play! "At about 6500 rpm, I change into third briefly on the small straight section before the final bend of the chicane, after which I accelerate towards the Seraglio bend, which I take in fifth. In the corner, the LC2 oversteers a little and the lateral acceleration is incredible; I'm travelling at 162 mph (260 km/h) and to exploit all of the track the left rear wheel goes off onto the grass. A corner full of excitement. I arrive very fast at the Roggia chicane and change down to second after

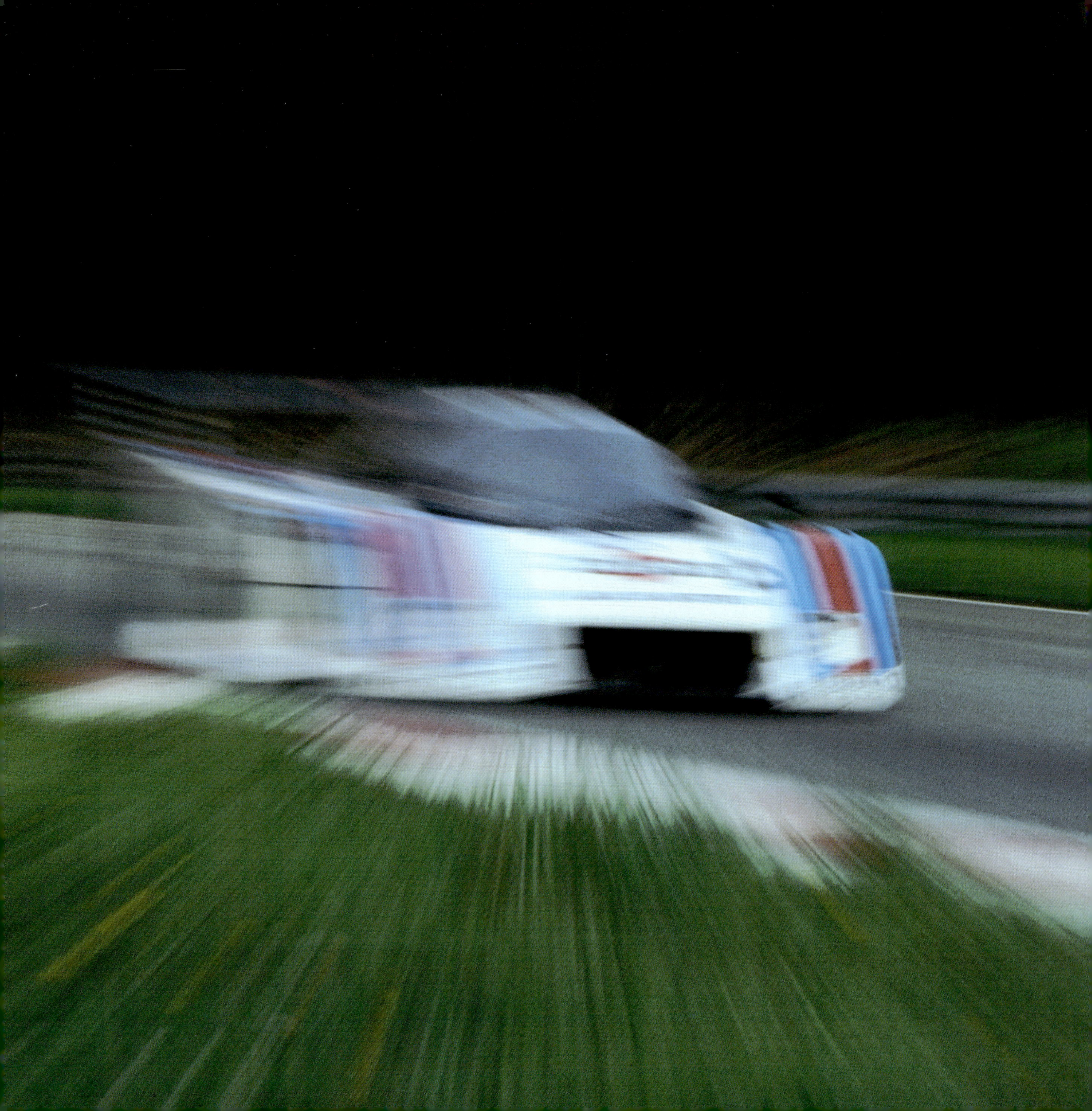

Monza, 1984: the LC2 playing the hare, hounded by a pack of Porsches.

decelerating; I move on for the first Lesmo bend (this was in 1987, ed.) which I take in fourth at over 118 mph (190 km/h), change again and press on until I clock 149 mph (240 km/h) exiting the second Lesmo curve". "Here, the LC2 does not understeer as it does in other slow corners and the centrifugal force takes me close to the internal shoulder. Before the underpass, I change into fifth to arrive at the deceleration point for Ascari at around 200 mph (320 km/h) before braking and changing into second, closing to the left. In the ample right-hander before the exit, the LC2 seems almost neutral. I take the pre-parabolica straight at full revs in third, touching the shoulder to exploit all of the track. I remain to the right, where there is the best asphalt, for subsequent braking. Then I change to fifth, but only for a few seconds because I'm coming up to the parabolica, which I take in third at about 112 mph (180 km/h). Where the asphalt changes colour (about mid-way through the bend) I change into fourth. In full acceleration I'm up to almost 150 mph (240 km/h) and I change to fifth losing 1800 rpm in the process (this happens as a result of most gear changes, ed.) and get up to 168 mph (270 km/h) at the pit wall … now jump out, because we have arrived".

Monza, 1984: a pit stop during practice.

Monza, 1986: the final works version of the LC2 going into the Ascari bend.

191

Printed by
Poligrafiche Bolis SpA, Bergamo, Italy,
in April 2001